Chocolate Cherry Tortes And Other Lowfat Delights

Maureen Egan and Penny Ballantyne

Bristol Publishing Enterprises
San Leandro, California

A Nitty Gritty® Cookbook

Printed in the United States of
America.

ISBN 0-911954-97-X

Cover photograph: Kathryn Opp
Food stylist: Carol Ladd
Cover graphics: Frank Paredes
Illustrator: Craig L. Davis

Table of Contents

We dedicate this book to our husbands,
Dave and Ford,
for their love and support through
yet another upheavel in our kitchens.
And to our children,
Jeffers, Hillary, Ford and Coco
for their willingness to try anything chocolate,
at least once.

Introduction

Chocolate, "Food of the gods!" Few of us are indifferent to its seductive lure. In fact, chocolate seems to have become a national addiction. Ironically, our consumption of chocolate hasn't lessened even with our commitment to health and fitness. In order to enjoy a chocolate dessert, many feel they have to "cheat" on their diets. Others simply abstain, believing that a prudent diet and fat-rich chocolate are incompatable.

Solid chocolate is rich in cocoa butter. It has 16 grams of fat per ounce, whereas cocoa has only 4 grams of fat per ounce—one fourth as much fat! Naturally, baking with solid chocolate adds a hefty amount of fat to a dessert. But here's the good news: desserts made with cocoa powder have significantly less fat than those made with solid chocolate.

Cocoa powder is manufactured by grinding roasted cacao beans, and heating them until the cocoa butter liquifies. The cocoa butter is then extracted from the "liquor," leaving a nearly fat-free powder. This powder is the essence of that chocolate taste so many of us crave.

We've created the recipes in this book to retain the wonderful taste of chocolate, while eliminating as much fat and cholesterol as possible without sacrificing taste and texture. Cocoa manufacturers recommend substituting three tablespoons of cocoa *plus* one tablespoon of a solid fat for each ounce of chocolate. Replacing solid chocolate with cocoa was, of course, a key concept in developing these recipes, yet we found it was not always necessary to add the fat to the conversion. Also, the fat content of cocoa varies somewhat from brand to brand. Carefully check over "gourmet" cocoa, as these tend to have a higher fat content. If you use a Dutched cocoa, replace any baking soda in a recipe with twice the amount of baking powder. We experimented with other lowfat ingredients to further scale down these recipes.

Even though eggs are a great source of protein, cholesterol is concentrated in the yolks. Over 230 milligrams per yolk! A healthy recommendation is to limit cholesterol to only 100 milligrams a day. In most of our recipes we've eliminated the yolks and used only the egg whites. Frozen egg substitutes work well in the recipes (read the labels, as certain brands may contain some fat!). Use them in the same measurement when whole eggs are called for.

Dairy products can be another source of additional fat and cholesterol. We've replaced high-fat cream, whole milk and cream cheese with healthier dairy products like skim milk, lowfat yogurt and buttermilk. The flavor and texture from using these products are so good that you'll never miss the fat!

It's important to get more fiber in our daily meals. Desserts can be a moderate source of fiber if some whole grains are used. Whenever possible, we like to use whole wheat pastry flour for half the total amount of flour called for in a recipe. By using a whole wheat pastry flour, cakes and cookies will have a more tender crumb than when using a coarser whole wheat bread flour. Definitely experiment with combinations of other grains such as oat, rye, triticale and buckwheat, to name a few.

All of the recipes in this book are under 200 calories and less than 8 grams of fat per serving. These desserts can be enjoyed by those following a prudent diet. Nutritional information per serving is listed at the end of each recipe, to help you calculate your daily intake of calories, fat and cholesterol.

Don't be afraid to experiment. Try these techniques to adapt your favorite chocolate recipes. Replace high-fat ingredients with healthy alternatives and create your own lowfat, delicious chocolate desserts.

CANDIES AND CONFECTIONS

Though the recipes in this chapter are lowfat versions of traditional candies, keep in mind that candy, even these healthier alternatives should be considered a treat and eaten in moderation. Is it possible to make chocolate candies without lots of solid chocolate, cream and huge amounts of sugar? We know it is.

Butter and pure chocolate are traditional ingredients used in candy making to impart creaminess and flavor. Some of the ingredients we've substituted, like potatoes and beans, may seem strange, but the delicious results will delight you.

When cooking any of the syrups, be sure to use a heavy-bottomed saucepan to prevent scorching. Divinity and seafoam should not be attempted on humid days, as they will absorb moisture from the air and remain sticky. If powdered milk is called for, process it in the food processor first. This makes the texture of the milk powder very fine. Candies and glazes made with this processed powdered milk will be smoother and creamier.

Finally, in order to insure that each piece of candy conforms to the nutritional information listed with the recipe, make the exact amount of candies specified.

Old-Fashioned Chocolate Taffy

50 pieces

Involve the whole family when making this candy. The extra hands will make pulling the taffy a lot easier!

1¼ cups sugar
⅓ cup cocoa
¼ cup water
¾ cup corn syrup

1 tbs. white vinegar
2 tsp. unsalted margarine
½ tsp. vanilla

In a heavy-bottomed saucepan, combine sugar, cocoa, water, corn syrup and vinegar. Cook mixture to 248°, or the firm ball stage. Pour the taffy into a 9" x 13" pan that has been sprayed with nonstick cooking spray. Cool until you can comfortably handle the taffy — it will still be quite warm and pliable. Oil your hands and start pulling and stretching the taffy. Fold it over and continue pulling and folding until the taffy lightens in color and becomes hard to pull. Pull it into ½" wide strips and cut into 1" pieces with an oiled scissors. Wrap each piece in a small square of waxed paper.

Nutritional information per serving   37 calories, .2 grams fat, 0 grams saturated fat, 0 mg cholesterol, .2 grams protein, 9 grams carbohydrate, 7 mg sodium

Chocolate Peppermint Seafoam

36 pieces

The peppermint candies give these a refreshing crunchy surprise. Don't add them until just before dropping onto the pans or the candy will melt.

½ cup corn syrup
2 cups brown sugar
½ cup water
1 tbs. white vinegar
2 egg whites
⅓ cup cocoa
¼ cup crushed peppermint candies, about 8 candies

In a heavy-bottomed saucepan, mix corn syrup, brown sugar, water and vinegar together and bring to a boil over medium heat. Boil mixture to 255° on a candy thermometer, or the hard ball stage. While sugar syrup is boiling, beat egg whites to soft peaks. Pour syrup over egg whites in a slow steady stream, whipping on medium speed. Increase speed to high and continue to whip for one minute. Reduce speed to low and add cocoa. Continue beating on high until mixture loses its glossy appearance and will hold its shape. Stir in the crushed candies. Drop by teaspoons onto a lightly greased cookie sheet. Cool completely at room temperature for several hours. Store in an airtight container. Don't attempt to make this candy on a humid day.

Nutritional information per serving 66 calories, 0 grams fat, 0 grams saturated fat, 0 mg cholesterol, .4 grams protein, 16 grams carbohydrate, 13 mg sodium

---

Chocolate-Mint Jellies

81 pieces

An unusual texture, and a wonderful fudgy taste. This is a sophisticated version of a familiar kid's treat.

1 cup skim milk
3 envelopes unflavored gelatin
1 cup lowfat buttermilk
2/3 cup brown sugar

1/2 cup cocoa
1/2 tsp. peppermint extract
2 tsp. sugar

In a small saucepan, sprinkle gelatin over skim milk to soften. In another saucepan, combine buttermilk, brown sugar and cocoa; heat to dissolve sugar. Set aside. Heat gelatin and milk over medium heat, stirring constantly until gelatin is dissolved. Stir this into chocolate mixture along with peppermint extract. Pour into a 9" x 9" pan that has been sprayed with nonstick cooking spray. Refrigerate until firm, about 4 hours. Cut into 81 squares and roll each in sugar. Store in a covered container in the refrigerator.

Nutritional information per serving 13 calories, 0 grams fat, 0 grams saturated fat, 0 mg cholesterol, 1 grams protein, 3 grams carbohydrate, 6 mg sodium

Chocolate Almond Truffles

The traditional truffle is made with lots of butter, solid chocolate and cream to give it body and texture. Don't despair, because we've devised an alternative to all that fat, so you can have guilt-free truffles. See if anyone can guess the secret ingredient in these delicious candies!

½ cup cooked or canned kidney beans,
  rinsed and drained
¼ cup lowfat ricotta cheese
½ cup powdered sugar

2½ tbs. cocoa
½ tsp. almond extract
¼ cup coarsely chopped almonds

In the mixing bowl of a food processor or blender, puree all ingredients except almonds until very smooth. If mixture is too soft to form balls easily, refrigerate until firm. Form into 36 balls. Roll each truffle into chopped almonds. Store in a covered container in the refrigerator. Truffles may also be frozen. Defrost twenty minutes before serving.

Nutritional information per serving   17 calories, .3 grams fat, .1 grams saturated fat, 0 mg cholesterol, 1 gram protein, 3 grams carbohydrate, 1 mg sodium

---

Fudge-Filled Dates

36 pieces

The fudge filling in these dates can also be used as a decorative icing. Just spoon it in a pastry bag fitted with a star tip and pipe it on anything for an artistic and delicious effect.

½ cup lowfat ricotta cheese
½ cup powdered sugar
5 tbs. cocoa

½ tsp. vanilla
36 whole pitted dates
2 tbs. powdered sugar

In a food processor or blender, combine ricotta cheese, powdered sugar, cocoa and vanilla. Process until very smooth and creamy. Spoon into a pastry bag fitted with a star tip. Pull dates open and pipe a ribbon of fudge mixture into center of each date. Store dates in a covered container in the refrigerator. Dust filled dates with powdered sugar just before serving.

Nutritional information per serving   31 calories, .6 grams fat, .2 grams saturated fat, 0 mg cholesterol, .7 grams protein, 7 grams carbohydrate, 2 mg sodium

Chocolate Divinity

36 pieces

Everyone will love this new twist on a traditional holiday candy.

2 cups sugar
½ cup corn syrup
½ cup water

2 egg whites
1 tsp. vanilla
⅓ cup cocoa

Mix sugar, corn syrup and water together in a heavy-bottomed saucepan and bring to a boil over medium heat. Boil mixture to 255° on a candy thermometer, or hard ball stage. While sugar syrup is boiling, beat egg whites to soft peaks. Pour syrup over egg whites in a slow, steady stream, whipping at medium speed. Increase speed to high and continue to whip for 1 minute. Reduce speed to low and add vanilla and cocoa. Continue beating on high until mixture loses its glossy appearance and holds its shape. Drop by teaspoons onto a lightly greased cookie sheet. Cool completely at room temperature for several hours. Store in an airtight container. Don't attempt to make this candy on a humid day.

Nutritional information per serving 60 calories, 0 grams fat, 0 grams saturated fat, 0 mg cholesterol, .4 grams protein, 15 grams carbohydrate, 9 mg sodium

Crunchy Pecan Squares

56 pieces

These crunchy confections have a rich, buttery flavor that melts in your mouth. They contain more fat than most of our other confections, but saturated fat is low, and only 24% of calories are from fat.

½ cup unsalted margarine
2 cups sugar
½ cup skim milk
2 cups old-fashioned oats

⅓ cup cocoa
½ cup ground pecans
1 tsp. vanilla

In a heavy bottomed saucepan, melt margarine and sugar in skim milk. Bring mixture to a boil, lower heat and continue to boil for three minutes. Remove from heat and stir in oats, cocoa, pecans and vanilla. Spread mixture in a 9" x 13" pan that has been sprayed with nonstick cooking spray. Cool at room temperature for 30 minutes; then cut into 56 pieces. Refrigerate until candy is hard. You may either store candy in a covered contained in the refrigerator or let it dry on a plate at room temperature for 4 to 6 hours.

Nutritional information per serving   60 calories, 2.5 grams fat, .4 grams saturated fat, 0 mg cholesterol, 1 gram protein, 9 grams carbohydrate, 1 mg sodium

Chocolate-Dipped Fruit

24 pieces

Dip only half the fruit into the glaze, allowing the freshness and color of the fruit to contrast with the dark chocolate. Strawberries with their stems intact are especially appealing.

1⅓ cup powdered sugar, sifted
¼ cup cocoa
1 egg white

3 tbs. skim milk
24 pieces of assorted fresh fruit

In a bowl, combine powdered sugar and cocoa. Add egg white and 2 tablespoons of skim milk. Beat until smooth and glossy, adding more milk if mixture is too thick. Dip fruit and allow glaze to set for thirty minutes. These do not store well, so eat them the same day they are made.

Nutritional information per serving   35 calories, .2 grams fat, 0 grams saturated fat, 0 mg cholesterol, .5 grams protein, 8 grams carbohydrate, 3 mg sodium

Chocolate Fondue

Servings: 12

A different, light dessert to serve a chocolate-loving crowd. Any firm, fresh fruit can be used for dipping. This is especially fun for a children's party.

3 tbs. cocoa
2 tbs. sugar
1 tsp. unsalted margarine
⅔ cup evaporated skim milk

1 tsp. vanilla
2 apples, each cored and sliced into
  12 pieces
12 fresh strawberries

In a saucepan, combine all ingredients except vanilla and fruit. Bring to a boil, stirring. Boil 2 minutes. Remove from heat and stir in vanilla. Pour into a fondue pot over low heat and surround with fruit.

Nutritional information per serving   49 calories, .7 grams fat, .1 grams saturated fat, 1 mg cholesterol, 2 grams protein, 10 grams carbohydrate, 16 mg sodium

Freezer Fudge

The dates lend additional sweetness, so less sugar is needed. Because the dates never freeze solid, this fudge remains chewy even when frozen.

1 cup dates, chopped
6 tbs. sugar
2 tsp. unsalted margarine

¼ cup cocoa
¾ cup skim milk
2 tsp. vanilla

In a food processor bowl, combine all ingredients except vanilla. Process until smooth. Pour contents into a small saucepan. Cook over medium heat for 5 minutes, stirring constantly. Remove from heat and add vanilla. Cool to lukewarm. Spoon into a lightly greased 8" x 8" pan. Freeze until firm. Cut in 2" x 1" pieces. Keep frozen until ready to serve.

Nutritional information per serving   30 calories, .4 grams fat, .1 grams saturated fat, 0 mg cholesterol, .5 grams protein, 7 grams carbohydrate, 3 mg sodium

Chocolate Spud Balls

20 pieces

Potatoes in candy? Yes, the potato adds moistness and body so less sugar and fat are needed. Delicious, and you'll fool everyone!

¾ cup mashed potatoes
6 tbs. cocoa
1 tsp. vanilla

1 cup powdered sugar
¼ cup ground almonds

In a bowl, mix mashed potatoes, cocoa, vanilla and powdered sugar. Let mixture set 15 minutes to firm up. Shape into 20 balls. Roll each into ground almonds. Store in a covered container in the refrigerator.

Nutritional information per serving 43 calories, .5 grams fat, .2 grams saturated fat, 0 mg cholesterol, 1 gram protein, 9 grams carbohydrate, 0 mg sodium

Mocha Balls

12 pieces

These candies have a rich coffee flavor with a slight hint of cinnamon.

½ tsp. cinnamon
½ tsp. cocoa
2 tsp. hot water
2 tsp. instant coffee

1 tbs. unsalted margarine
6 tbs. cocoa
¼ cup honey
½ cup processed nonfat milk powder

In a small bowl, combine cinnamon and ½ tsp. cocoa. Set aside. In a saucepan, dissolve coffee in water. Add margarine, remaining cocoa and honey. Stir over low heat to melt margarine and blend ingredients. Remove from heat and stir in powdered milk, kneading in last amount to form a dough. Shape into 12 balls. Roll in cinnamon-cocoa mixture. Store in a covered container in the refrigerator.

Nutritional information per serving 59 calories, 1 gram fat, .5 grams saturated fat, 1 mg cholesterol, 3 grams protein, 10 grams carbohydrate, 26 mg sodium

Molded Chocolate Candies

12 pieces

Solid chocolate used for molding contains a very high percentage of fat, up to 35%! We've devised a recipe with a bare minimum of fat using cocoa instead of chocolate.

½ cup sugar
3 tbs. cocoa
2 tsp. corn syrup

¼ cup evaporated skim milk
1 tsp. unsalted margarine
½ tsp. vanilla

In a heavy-bottomed saucepan, combine all ingredients except vanilla. Cook over low heat 5 minutes, stirring occasionally. Remove from heat and cool to lukewarm. Add vanilla and beat 1 minute. Spray 12 individual 2" candy molds with nonstick cooking spray. Pour mixture evenly into molds. Freeze until firm. Rap molds upside down on the counter to dislodge candies, or carefully pry out with a knife point. Store in a covered container.

Nutritional information per serving 48 calories, .6 grams fat, 0 grams saturated fat, 0 mg cholesterol, 1 gram protein, 10 grams carbohydrate, 6 mg sodium

---

Rum Balls

Rum balls are a perfect candy to whip up for the holidays — they're a snap to make, naturally low in fat and delicious. Be sure to try the maple-nut variation.

1½ cups vanilla wafer crumbs
¼ cup ground almonds
2 tbs. cocoa
¼ cup corn syrup

1 tbs. water
½ tsp. rum extract
4 tsp. powdered sugar

In a bowl, combine crumbs, ground almonds and cocoa. Stir in corn syrup, water and rum extract to make a smooth dough. Shape into 16 balls. Roll lightly in powdered sugar. Store in a covered container.

Variation

Maple-Nut Chocolate Balls. Substitute maple syrup for corn syrup and vanilla extract for rum extract. Roll balls in cocoa instead of powdered sugar.

Nutritional information per serving   44 calories, 1.6 grams fat, 0 grams saturated fat, 0 mg cholesterol, 3 grams protein, 7 grams carbohydrate, 18 mg sodium

Monkey Bars

12 pieces

This is a funny name for a fun treat. Let the kids help make these easy and quick no-cook confections.

6 tbs. peanut butter, sugarless
3 tbs. powdered sugar
3 tbs. processed nonfat milk powder
2 whole graham crackers (5 tbs. crumbs)
4-5 tsp. water

In a small bowl, mix together peanut butter, powdered sugar and powdered milk until smooth. Stir in cracker crumbs and 4 teaspoons water. If mixture is too dry, add additional water to make a firm dough. Shape into 12 logs. Dip tops in chocolate glaze. Store in a covered container in the refrigerator.

Chocolate Glaze

1 tbs. cocoa
1 tbs. powdered sugar
1 tbs. processed nonfat milk powder
2 tsp. hot water

In a small bowl, combine ingredients and mix until smooth.

Nutritional information per serving 73 calories, 4 grams fat, 1 gram saturated fat, 0 mg cholesterol, 3 grams protein, 7 grams carbohydrate, 30 mg sodium

---

Crunchy Chocolate Squares

36 pieces

You can use any type of cereal, just be sure it's a low sugar variety.

¾ cup sugar
6 tbs. cocoa
1½ tbs. cornstarch
6 tbs. evaporated skim milk

1½ tsp. unsalted margarine
½ tsp. vanilla
¾ cup sugarless flake cereal

In a saucepan, combine all ingredients except vanilla and cereal. Cook over low heat 5 minutes, stirring occasionally. Remove from heat and cool slightly. Stir in vanilla and cereal. Spread into a lightly greased 8" x 8" pan. Chill until set. Cut into 36 squares. Store in a covered container in the refrigerator.

Nutritional information per serving 25 calories, .3 grams fat, 0 grams saturated fat, 0 mg cholesterol, 1 gram protein, 6 grams carbohydrate, 4 mg sodium

Granola Bars

Cocoa adds an interesting taste to these nutritious bars.

1½ cups old-fashioned oats
¼ cup sunflower seeds
¼ cup cashews, chopped
¼ cup vegetable oil

⅓ cup honey
3 tbs. cocoa
½ tsp. vanilla

Toast oats in an ungreased pan at 350° for 10 minutes. Place oats in a bowl and stir in sunflower seeds and cashews. In a small saucepan, heat oil, honey and cocoa, stirring to mix. Remove from heat and add vanilla. Pour over oat mixture. Mix well. With wetted fingers, press mixture firmly into a lightly greased 7" x 11" pan. Bake at 350° for 12 to 15 minutes. Let cool 5 minutes. Score into 16 bars and allow to cool completely. Break bars along the score lines.

Nutritional information per serving 98 calories, 5.6 grams fat, .7 grams saturated fat, 0 mg cholesterol, 2 grams protein, 11 grams carbohydrate, 0 mg sodium

Chocolate Mint Cremes

12 pieces

Mint and chocolate are a natural together. These creamy confections use powdered milk instead of all sugar to thicken the mints.

3 oz. Neufchatel cheese
8 tbs. processed nonfat milk powder
1/4 cup powdered sugar
1/2 tsp. mint extract
2 tbs. powdered sugar

In a small bowl, combine Neufchatel cheese, dry milk, 1/4 cup powdered sugar and mint extract. Freeze mixture 10 minutes to firm up. Remove from freezer and form into 12 balls, using powdered sugar to coat hands. Refreeze for 20 minutes or until almost hard. Remove from freezer and press balls into patties. Spread chocolate glaze over tops of each mint. Store in a covered container in the refrigerator. They can also be frozen.

Chocolate Glaze

¼ cup powdered sugar
1 tbs. cocoa
1 tsp. unsalted margarine
1 tsp. skim milk

In a small saucepan, combine all ingredients. Heat to melt margarine and use while warm.

Nutritional information per serving 63 calories, 2 grams fat, 1 gram saturated fat, 6 mg cholesterol, 3 grams protein, 9 grams carbohydrate, 51 mg sodium

Cookies and Bars

To increase the nutritional value of the cookies you make, try experimenting with various flours and grains. Cookies lend themselves well to experimentation. Substitute rolled oats, cornmeal, oat or wheat bran for a portion of the flour. Rye flour, whole wheat pastry flour or defatted soy flour can also be used. These combinations will result in interesting new flavors and textures, while giving your cookies a real nutritional boost.

To eliminate additional fat and calories (as well as making clean-up a snap!) line the cookie sheets with parchment paper instead of greasing them. The cookies will practically slide off the sheet, and the paper can be thrown away.

Cool bars from the oven on a cooling rack. Then cut the bars into the recommended number of pieces listed in the recipe.

Fudgy Brownies

Chocolate fanciers are crazy about brownies. These are iced with a rich chocolate icing.

¼ cup whole wheat pastry flour
½ cup unbleached white flour
½ cup *plus* 2 tbs. sugar
¼ cup cocoa

3 egg whites
¼ cup vegetable oil
1 tsp. vanilla

In a large bowl, sift dry ingredients; set aside. In a small bowl, combine egg whites, oil and vanilla. Add to dry ingredients. Pour into a lightly greased 8"x8" pan. Bake at 350° for 18 to 20 minutes. *Don't overbake.* When cool, ice brownies.

Icing

⅔ cup powdered sugar
2 tbs. cocoa

1 tbs. unsalted margarine
2-3 tsp. skim milk

In a small bowl, cream all ingredients together, adding more milk if necessary to make a smooth icing.

Nutritional information per serving 117 calories, 4 grams fat, 1 gram saturated fat, 0 mg cholesterol, 2 grams protein, 18 grams carbohydrate, 35 mg sodium

Sugarless Brownies

16 bars

An unbelievably delicious, moist brownie without any sugar! For the smoothest icing, first process the powdered milk until very fine.

¾ cup chopped dates (about 20)
½ cup whole wheat pastry flour
¼ cup cocoa
½ tsp. baking soda
2 tbs. water

6 tbs. unsweetened apple-raspberry
 juice concentrate, thawed
1½ tsp. vanilla
3 egg whites
¼ cup vegetable oil

In a food processor, process dates, flour and cocoa until finely ground. Add baking soda. In a bowl, combine wet ingredients and stir into flour-date mixture. Pour into a lightly greased 8"x8" pan and bake at 350° for 23 minutes. Cool and ice.

Icing

2 oz. Neufchatel cheese
2½ tsp. unsweetened apple juice
 concentrate, thawed

1½ tbs. cocoa
2 tbs. nonfat dry milk powder

In a medium bowl, combine all ingredients and beat with an electric mixer until smooth.

Nutritional information per serving 114 calories, 5 grams fat, 1 gram saturated fat, 3 mg cholesterol, 2 grams protein, 17 grams carbohydrate, 54 mg sodium

Marbles

24 cookies

The twisting and rounding of the dough produces a marbled effect.

⅓ cup unsalted margarine
⅓ cup sugar
1 egg white
½ tsp. vanilla

1 cup unbleached flour
¼ tsp. baking powder
1 tbs. cocoa

In a large bowl, cream margarine and sugar. Beat in egg white and vanilla. Sift flour and baking powder and beat into creamed mixture. Add cocoa to ½ of the dough. Roll each half into a log one foot long and twist together. Chill in freezer 15 minutes. Cut log into 24 pieces, roll each piece into a ball and place on a cookie sheet lined with parchment paper. Flatten cookies slightly. Bake at 375° for 8 to 10 minutes.

Nutritional information per serving 52 calories, 3 grams fat, 0 grams saturated fat, 0 mg cholesterol, 1 gram protein, 6 grams carbohydrate, 57 mg sodium

Sugarless Chocolate Cookies

20 cookies

You will never believe that this crisp, iced cookie is made without any sugar!

1 cup whole wheat pastry flour
½ cup toasted wheat germ
¼ cup cocoa
1 tsp. baking powder
½ tsp. baking soda

6 tbs. unsweetened apple juice
  concentrate, thawed
¼ cup unsalted margarine
1 tsp. vanilla

In a large bowl, combine dry ingredients. Add remaining ingredients and mix to form a dough. Roll out ⅛" thick on a floured surface. Cut out cookies with a 3" cutter. Place on a cookie sheet lined with parchment paper and bake at 350° for 12 minutes. Cool and ice.

Icing

⅓ cup nonfat dry milk powder
3 tbs. unsweetened apple juice
  concentrate, thawed

1 tbs. cocoa
1 tbs. unsalted margarine

In a food processor, process powdered milk until fine. Beat in remaining ingredients until smooth.

Nutritional information per serving 82 calories, 3 grams fat, 1 gram saturated fat, 0 mg cholesterol, 3 grams protein, 11 grams carbohydrate, 52 mg sodium

Chocolate Cut-Outs

24 cookies

For a change, try this chocolate version of sugar cookies.

⅓ cup sugar
¼ cup vegetable oil
2 egg whites
2 tbs. skim milk
1 tsp. vanilla

1 cup unbleached white flour
½ cup whole wheat pastry flour
¼ cup cocoa
1 tsp. baking powder
2½ tbs. chopped almonds

In a large bowl, combine first five ingredients. Sift dry ingredients, except almonds and add to bowl. Mix well. Chill dough 15 minutes in freezer. Roll out on a floured surface to ⅛" thick. Cut out cookies with a 3" cutter. Place on a cookie sheet lined with parchment paper. Sprinkle almonds over tops of cookies. Bake at 350° for 10 to 12 minutes.

Nutritional information per serving 67 calories, 3 grams fat, 0 grams saturated fat, 0 mg cholesterol, 3 grams protein, 9 grams carbohydrate, 3 mg sodium

Cherry Chocolate Drops

30 cookies

There is just a subtle hint of cherries in these plump, cake-like cookies.

1/3 cup unsalted margarine
1/2 cup sugar
2 egg whites
1/4 cup cocoa
1/8 tsp. almond extract
3/4 cup whole wheat pastry flour
3/4 cup unbleached white flour
1/2 tsp. baking powder
1/2 tsp. baking soda
1/2 cup lowfat buttermilk
1/2 cup sour cherries, drained, juice reserved, towel-dried, finely chopped

In a large bowl, cream margarine, sugar and egg whites. Beat in cocoa and almond extract. Sift flours with baking powder and soda; add to creamed mixture alternately with buttermilk. Stir in cherries. Drop by teaspoon onto a cookie sheet lined with parchment paper. Bake at 350° for 10 to 12 minutes. Glaze while cookies are still warm.

Cherry Glaze

¾ cup powdered sugar
3-4 tsp. reserved cherry juice
⅛ tsp. almond extract

In a small bowl, blend ingredients together, adding more cherry juice if necessary to make a smooth icing.

Nutritional information per serving 69 calories, 2 grams fat, 0 grams saturated fat, 0 mg cholesterol, 1 gram protein, 11 grams carbohydrate, 28 mg sodium

Chocolate-Striped Peanut Cookies

30 cookies

Here's a special treat for those who like a little peanut butter with their chocolate.

¼ cup sugarless peanut butter
2 tbs. unsalted margarine
⅓ cup brown sugar
¼ cup unsweetened apple juice
  concentrate, thawed

2 egg whites
¾ cup unbleached white flour
½ cup whole wheat pastry flour
¾ tsp. baking soda

In a large bowl, cream peanut butter and margarine. Add brown sugar and juice; cream well. Stir in egg whites. Sift flours with baking soda and add to creamed mixture. Mix until well blended. Chill dough. Drop by teaspoons onto a cookie sheet lined with parchment paper and flatten slightly. Bake at 350° for 10 to 12 minutes. Cool. Thinly ice bottoms of cookies and let dry. Turn and pipe stripes on tops of cookies.

Icing

⅔ cup powdered sugar
2 tbs. cocoa

1 tbs. unsalted margarine
2-3 tsp. skim milk

In a small bowl, combine all ingredients until well blended, adding more milk if necessary to make a smooth icing.

Nutritional information per serving 64 calories, 2 grams fat, 0 grams saturated fat, 0 mg cholesterol, 1 gram protein, 10 grams carbohydrate, 27 mg sodium

Fudge Drops

36 cookies

These gems are dairy-less and egg-less. Tofu provides the smooth texture.

8 ozs. firm tofu
1/4 cup vegetable oil
2/3 cup sugar
6 tbs. cocoa
1 cup whole wheat pastry flour

3/4 cup unbleached white flour
3/4 tsp. baking soda
1 tsp. vanilla
2 1/2 tsp. sugar

In a food processor, blend tofu and oil until smooth. Add sugar, cocoa, flours, soda and vanilla, blending after each addition. Dough will be stiff. Put 2 1/2 tsp. sugar in a small bowl. Drop dough by teaspoons into sugar to coat. Place on a cookie sheet lined with parchment paper. Press cookies with the bottom of a glass, or use wetted fingers to flatten. Bake at 350° for 10 to 12 minutes.

Nutritional information per serving   59 calories, 2 grams fat, 0 grams saturated fat, 0 mg cholesterol, 1 gram protein, 9 grams carbohydrate, 17 mg sodium

Chocolate Cheese Bars

9 bars

These rich bars are best served the same day they are made.

Crust

½ cup unbleached white flour
2 tbs. brown sugar
¼ cup quick oats
1 tbs. unsalted margarine

2 tbs. unsweetened apple juice
  concentrate, thawed
1 cup fresh strawberries

In a medium bowl, combine flour, brown sugar and oats. Cut in margarine and juice. Press into a lightly greased 8"x8" pan. Bake at 350° for 5 to 7 minutes until crust just begins to brown. Cool slightly; pour filling over crust. Bake at 350° for 25 minutes. Cool to room temperature before refrigerating. Before serving, top each piece with a strawberry.

Filling

3 ozs. neufchatel cheese
½ cup 1% dry cottage cheese
3 tbs. cocoa
1 egg white

¼ cup sugar
¼ cup lowfat buttermilk
3 tbs. unsweetened apple juice
concentrate, thawed

In a medium bowl, beat cheeses with cocoa, egg white and sugar until smooth. Stir in buttermilk and juice.

Nutritional information per serving   137 calories, 4 grams fat, 2 grams saturated fat, 8 mg cholesterol, 5 grams protein, 21 grams carbohydrate, 53 mg sodium

Ice Cream Sandwiches

Keep a supply of these cookies in the freezer for a cool treat on hot summer days.

1/3 cup honey
1/4 cup vegetable oil
2 egg whites
3/4 cup unsweetened applesauce
1 cup whole wheat pastry flour

1/2 cup unbleached white flour
1 tsp. baking soda
2 tsp. vanilla
2 1/2 cups lowfat ice milk

In a large bowl, beat together honey, oil, egg whites and applesauce. Sift flours and soda; add with vanilla and mix until smooth. Drop 20 cookies on a cookie sheet lined with parchment paper. Press with wetted fingers to flatten. Bake at 350° for 10 to 12 minutes. Cool. Place 1/4 cup ice milk between two cookies, bottoms together. Wrap tightly with plastic wrap and freeze.

Nutritional information per serving 199 calories, 7 grams fat, 1 gram saturated fat, 4 mg cholesterol, 4 grams protein, 32 grams carbohydrate, 120 mg sodium

Oatmeal Meringue Cookies

36 cookies

These tasty cookies have a wonderful crunch.

3 egg whites
⅔ cup brown sugar
4 tbs. cocoa
¼ tsp. cream of tartar

1 tsp. vanilla
2½ cups oatmeal
¼ cup chopped pecans
¼ cup raisins

In a small bowl, combine brown sugar and cocoa and set aside. In a large mixing bowl, beat egg whites until foamy and add cream of tartar. Continue beating on high speed, adding sugar-cocoa mixture by tablespoons until meringue holds stiff, glossy peaks. Do not underbeat. Add vanilla. Carefully fold in nuts, oatmeal and raisins. Drop by teaspoonfuls onto a baking sheet sprayed with nonstick cooking spray. Bake at 350° for 10 to 15 minutes or until cookies feel dry. Cool on a rack.

Nutritional information per serving 50 calories, 1 gram fat, 0 grams saturated fat, 0 mg cholesterol, 2 grams protein, 8 grams carbohydrate, 0 mg sodium

---

Chocolate Marble Cheesecake Bars

16 bars

These bars are moist and delicious and pretty as well.

Batter 1

6 ozs. lowfat ricotta cheese
2 egg whites
1/4 cup sugar

1 tsp. vanilla
2 tbs. flour

In a mixing bowl, combine all ingredients and beat on medium speed for 1 to 2 minutes. Set aside.

Batter 2

3/4 cup flour
3/4 cup sugar
4 tbs. cocoa
1/2 tsp. baking soda

1/3 cup lowfat buttermilk
1/4 cup margarine, melted
2 egg whites
1 tsp. vanilla

In a medium bowl, combine flour, sugar, cocoa and baking soda and set aside. In a mixing bowl, beat together egg whites, buttermilk, margarine and vanilla, add dry ingredients and beat at medium speed 1 minute. Pour into a 9"x9" pan which has been sprayed with nonstick cooking spray. Spoon Batter 1 in pools on top and swirl two batters together with the blade of a knife. Bake at 350° for 45 minutes or until a cake tester comes out clean. Cool in the pan.

Nutritional information per serving 123 calories, 4 grams fat, 1 gram saturated fat, 1 mg cholesterol, 3 grams protein, 18 grams carbohydrate, 59 mg sodium

Chocolate Molasses Crisps

36 cookies

Here's a variation on an old favorite.

½ cup margarine, melted
½ cup white sugar
½ cup brown sugar
⅓ cup molasses
2 egg whites, lightly beaten
1¾ cups unbleached white flour

2 tsp. baking soda
¼ cup cocoa
1¼ tsp. cinnamon
¼ tsp. *each* allspice, nutmeg, ginger
white sugar to coat cookies

In a large bowl, combine margarine and sugars. Add molasses and egg whites and beat well. In another bowl, combine flour, baking soda, cocoa and spices; add to molasses mixture. Form into 1" balls and roll in additional granulated sugar. Place on a lightly greased cookie sheet and flatten slightly. Bake at 375° for 7 to 8 minutes. Cool on a wire rack.

Nutritional information per serving 74 calories, 3 grams fat, .5 grams saturated fat, 0 mg cholesterol, 1 gram protein, 12 grams carbohydrate, 48 mg sodium

Chocolate Oatmeal Cookies

36 cookies

These cookies are real kid-pleasers, and good for them too!

½ cup unsalted margarine, softened
¾ cup brown sugar
½ cup white sugar
2 egg whites
1 tsp. vanilla

1 cup unbleached white flour
½ cup whole wheat flour
1 tsp. baking soda
3 cups oatmeal
4 tbs. cocoa

In a mixing bowl, combine margarine and sugars and beat until well blended. Add egg whites and vanilla and beat until mixture is light and fluffy, about 2 minutes. In another bowl, mix flours, baking soda and cocoa. Add dry ingredients to wet ingredients and blend well. Add oatmeal and any additions listed, blend and drop by rounded teaspoonfuls onto a lightly greased cookie sheet. Bake at 350° for 10 to 12 minutes.

Variations: add 1 tsp. cinnamon and ¼ tsp. nutmeg; or ½ cup raisins; or ½ cup chopped dates; or ¼ cup wheat germ; or ¼ cup sunflower seeds.

Nutritional information per serving 87 calories, 3 grams fat, .5 grams saturated fat, 0 mg cholesterol, 2 grams protein, 14 grams carbohydrate, 25 mg sodium

Fudge Crackles

36 cookies

These rich, fudgy cookies will disappear nearly as fast as you make them!

½ cup margarine, melted
6 tbs. cocoa
1 cup sugar
2 egg whites

1½ tsp. vanilla
2 cups flour
2 tsp. baking powder
powdered sugar

In a bowl, combine margarine and cocoa. Add sugar, egg whites and vanilla. In another bowl, combine flour and baking powder; add to wet ingredients and beat well. Shape into 1" balls and roll in powdered sugar. Place on a baking sheet which has been sprayed with nonstick spray. Bake at 350° for 8 minutes. Cookies should still be soft when removed from oven. Cool on a wire rack.

Nutritional information per serving 71 calories, 3 grams fat, .5 grams saturated fat, 0 mg cholesterol, 1 gram protein, 11 grams carbohydrate, 15 mg sodium

Mocha Rum Brownies

16 bars

Everyone's favorite is brownies, and this is a delicious variation.

½ cup unsalted margarine
1 cup sugar
2 egg whites
1 tsp. instant coffee dissolved in
  2 tsp. boiling water
½ tsp. rum flavoring

¾ cup unbleached white flour
6 tbs. cocoa
¼ tsp. baking powder
½ cup skim milk
powdered sugar, fresh strawberry
  halves (optional)

In a mixing bowl, combine margarine and sugar. Add egg whites and beat until light and fluffy, about 2 or 3 minutes. In another bowl, mix flour, cocoa and baking powder. Add to wet ingredients alternately with milk, stirring until well blended. Spread in a 9"x9" pan which has been sprayed with nonstick cooking spray and bake at 350° for 25 minutes. Cool in pan. Dust with powdered sugar before serving and garnish with strawberry halves if desired.

Nutritional information per serving 131 calories, 6 grams fat, 1 gram saturated fat, 0 mg cholesterol, 2 grams protein, 17 grams carbohydrate, 13 mg sodium

Chocolate Applesauce Bars

16 bars

Pack these in your fall picnic or tailgate party basket.

¾ cup sugar
1¼ cups unbleached white flour
¼ cup cocoa
1 tsp. baking soda
1 tsp. cinnamon

¼ cup oil
¾ cup unsweetened applesauce
2 egg whites
1 tsp. vanilla
⅓ cup chopped walnuts

In a medium bowl, combine sugar, flour, cocoa, baking soda and cinnamon. In a mixing bowl, combine cocoa, oil, applesauce, egg whites and vanilla; beat at medium speed 2 minutes. Add dry ingredients and mix just to combine. Spread in a 9"x9" pan that has been sprayed with nonstick cooking spray. Sprinkle nuts on top and bake at 350° for 20 to 25 minutes. Cool in the pan.

Nutritional information per serving   127 calories, 5 grams fat, .5 grams saturated fat, 0 mg cholesterol, 6 grams protein, 18 grams carbohydrate, 57 mg sodium

Raspberry Fudge Bars

24 bars

The raspberry topping and chocolate flavor make a delicious combination in this treat.

1½ cups unbleached white flour
½ cup cocoa
1 tsp. baking soda
1 cup lowfat buttermilk
½ cup oil

1 cup sugar
4 egg whites
1 tsp. vanilla
1 (10 ozs.) jar all fruit red raspberry
    spread

In a bowl, combine flour, cocoa and baking soda; set aside. In a large bowl, combine buttermilk, oil, sugar, egg whites and vanilla. Beat at medium speed 2 minutes. Add dry ingredients and mix until well blended. Spread in a 9"x13" pan that has been sprayed with nonstick cooking spray. Melt raspberry spread in a microwave oven or in a pan over simmering water. With a spoon, dribble jam over batter. Bake at 350° for 30 to 35 minutes. Cool in pan.

Nutritional information per serving 147 calories, 5 grams fat, .6 grams saturated fat, 0 mg cholesterol, 2 grams protein, 25 grams carbohydrate, 21 mg sodium

Chocolate Pumpkin Bars

24 bars

Try these for a Halloween treat.

Pumpkin Layer

3 egg whites
2/3 cup evaporated skim milk
3/4 cup sugar
1 tsp. cinnamon

1/4 tsp. ginger
1/4 tsp. nutmeg
1/8 tsp. cloves
2 cups canned pumpkin

Cake Layer

2 1/4 cups flour
1/2 cup cocoa
1 1/2 tsp. baking soda
1 cup sugar

1/2 cup oil
3 egg whites
1 cup reserved pumpkin mixture

Prepare the pumpkin layer first. In a large bowl, beat egg whites, evaporated skim milk, sugar, spices and pumpkin at medium speed about 1 minute until well blended. Remove 1 cup of mixture; set both aside. In another bowl, combine flour, cocoa, baking soda, sugar, oil, egg whites and reserved pumpkin mixture. Beat on medium speed to combine; beat on high speed 2 minutes. Pour into a 9"x13" pan that has been sprayed with nonstick cooking spray and spread pumpkin mixture on top. Bake at 350° for 40 to 45 minutes. Cool in pan.

Nutritional information per serving   158 calories, 5 grams fat, .6 grams saturated fat, 0 mg cholesterol, 3 grams protein, 26 grams carbohydrate, 88 mg sodium

Oat Fudge Bars

12 bars

A chocolate fudge filling is sandwiched between sweet oatmeal crusts.

Crust

1 cup quick oats
½ cup unbleached white flour
¼ cup brown sugar
¼ tsp. baking soda

3 tbs. unsalted margarine
1 egg white
2 tbs. unsweetened apple juice
  concentrate, thawed

In a medium bowl, combine dry ingredients. Cut in remaining ingredients until crumbly. Press two thirds of mixture into a lightly greased 7"x11" crust. Bake at 350° for 10 minutes. Cool slightly. Spread filling over crust. Dot with remaining dough. Bake at 350° for 20 minutes until top is light brown.

Filling

3 tbs. unsalted margarine
¼ cup sugar
2 tbs. unsweetened apple juice
  concentrate
3 tbs. cocoa

1 egg white
¼ cup unbleached white flour
¼ tsp. baking powder
¼ cup skim milk
1 tsp. vanilla

In a small saucepan, melt margarine with sugar and juice. Remove from heat and stir in remaining ingredients in order given, mixing well.

Nutritional information per serving 143 calories, 6 grams fat, 1 gram saturated fat, 0 mg cholesterol, 3 grams protein, 20 grams carbohydrate, 45 mg sodium

Chocolate Almond Kisses

36 cookies

Kiss the cook! This fat-free delight only has 16 calories!

⅔ cup powdered sugar
⅓ cup cocoa
3 egg whites

¼ tsp. cream of tartar
¼ tsp almond extract
¼ cup coarsely ground almonds

In a small bowl, combine powdered sugar and cocoa; set aside. In a large mixing bowl, beat egg whites until foamy and add cream of tartar. Continue beating on high speed, adding cocoa-sugar mixture by the tablespoonful until stiff glossy peaks form. Do not underbeat. Add almond extract and gently fold in ground almonds. Drop by teaspoonfuls onto cookie sheets sprayed with non-stick cooking spray. Bake at 350° for 10 to 15 minutes or until surface of cookies feels dry. Cool on wire racks.

Nutritional information per serving   16 calories, 0 grams fat, 0 grams saturated fat, 0 mg cholesterol, 1 gram protein, 3 grams carbohydrate, 0 mg sodium

Cakes

When making cakes, start by having all ingredients at room temperature. This aids in the mixing process and ensures a smooth batter. Egg whites will whip to a greater volume when they are warm, rather than straight from the refrigerator. It is important to sift the dry ingredients together when noted in the recipe. Otherwise, the leavening agent won't be evenly distributed and the cake will have poor volume.

Use your food processor for a quick and easy way to mix cake batters. Follow the manufacturer's instructions for preparing cakes. You can even whip egg whites in your processor if you have a special whip attachment. To help remove cakes from the pans, use parchment or waxed paper to line the bottom of the cake pan. Cut the paper to fit the inside bottom of the pan. Lightly spray the pan with a nonstick cooking spray and place the paper inside.

Always preheat the oven to the temperature recommended in the recipe. Cakes are done when the middle springs back lightly when touched, or a cake tester inserted in the middle of the cake comes out clean. Cool cakes in the pan on a rack until they reach room temperature. Then invert cakes to remove from the pans and finish cooling on racks, right side up. Be sure to remove the paper liner before transferring the cake to a serving plate. If you plan to freeze the cake, leave the paper liner on to help seal in moisture and give the cake some stability. Remove the liner when the cake is defrosted.

Marble Cake

This cake is quick and easy to make, and it keeps well, too.

2 cups unbleached white flour
1 cup *plus* 1 tbs. sugar
3½ tsp. baking powder
½ cup vegetable oil
4 egg whites

1 cup skim milk
1 tsp. vanilla
1½ tbs. cocoa
1½ tbs. warm water

In a large bowl, mix together flour, 1 cup sugar, baking powder, oil, 2 egg whites and ½ cup of milk. Beat on low speed with a mixer until well blended. Beat 2 minutes on high speed. Add remaining milk, egg whites and vanilla and beat 2 more minutes. In a small bowl, mix cocoa, 1 tbs. sugar and 1 tbs. warm water until blended. Add ½ cup of white batter to cocoa mixture and mix well. Spray a 9"x13" pan with nonstick cooking spray and pour in white batter. Place spoonfuls of cocoa batter on top and swirl with the blade of a knife. Bake at 350° for 20 minutes or until a cake tester comes out clean.

Nutritional information per serving 172 calories, 7 grams fat, .6 grams saturated fat, 0 mg cholesterol, 3 grams protein, 24 grams carbohydrate, 92 mg sodium

Chocolate Cheesecake

Servings: 12

This creamy, rich cheesecake is light too.

1 cup sugar
3 tbs. flour
4 tbs. cocoa
4 cups lowfat ricotta cheese
1/2 cup lowfat buttermilk

1 egg *plus* 4 egg whites or egg
  substitute equal to 4 eggs
2 tsp. vanilla
Graham Cracker Crust #1, page 90

In a small bowl, mix sugar, flour and cocoa. In a food processor, blend ricotta, buttermilk, eggs and vanilla. Add cocoa-sugar mixture and process until smooth and creamy. Pour into cooled crust and bake at 375° for 45 minutes or until center is set. Cool.

Nutritional information per serving   181 calories, 5 grams fat, .5 grams saturated fat, 0 mg cholesterol, 11 grams protein, 28 grams carbohydrate, 266 mg sodium

Chocolate Pound Cake

Servings: 16

This pound cake won't add pounds!

½ cup unsalted margarine
¾ cup sugar
3 egg whites
1¾ cups unbleached white flour
⅓ cup cocoa

1¼ tsp. baking soda
8 ozs. lowfat vanilla yogurt
1 tsp. almond extract
1 tbs. vanilla extract

In a large bowl, beat softened margarine and sugar until light lemon colored. Add egg whites and beat until mixture is light and fluffy. Mix flour, cocoa and soda; add to margarine mixture alternately with yogurt. Blend well; add vanilla and almond flavorings. Spray an 8"x3" loaf pan with nonstick cooking spray. Pour batter into pan and bake at 350° for 50 to 60 minutes or until a cake tester inserted in the center comes out clean. Invert on a wire rack to cool.

Nutritional information per serving 150 calories, 6 grams fat, 1 gram saturated fat, 1 mg cholesterol, 3 grams protein, 20 grams carbohydrate, 82 mg sodium

Quick Fudge Pudding Cake

Servings: 12

Here's a wonderful variation on a old favorite.

1 cup unbleached white flour
1/2 cup white sugar
1/4 cup *plus* 2 tbs. cocoa
2 tsp. baking powder
1/2 cup nonfat milk

2 tbs. unsalted margarine, melted
1 tsp. vanilla
1/2 tsp. almond extract
3/4 cup brown sugar
1 3/4 cups hot water

In a large bowl, combine flour, white sugar, 2 tbs. cocoa and baking powder. Add milk, margarine, vanilla and almond extract; blend well. Pour into a 9"x9" ungreased pan. Mix brown sugar with 1/4 cup cocoa and sprinkle evenly over top. Pour hot water over brown sugar. Bake at 350° for 40 to 45 minutes. Cool slightly and serve warm.

Nutritional information per serving   145 calories, 2 grams fat, .6 grams saturated fat, 0 mg cholesterol, 2 grams protein, 30 grams carbohydrate, 42 mg sodium

Chocolate Mint Angel Food Cake

Servings: 12

This cake is light as a cloud, but full of flavor.

¾ cup white flour, sifted
¼ cup cocoa
¼ cup sugar
12 egg whites

1¼ tsp. cream of tartar
1 cup sugar
1½ tsp. vanilla
⅓ cup crushed peppermint candies

Sift flour, cocoa and ¼ cup sugar and set aside. Beat egg whites until foamy and add cream of tartar. Continue beating on high speed, adding remaining cup of sugar 2 tablespoons at a time until stiff, glossy peaks form. Add vanilla. Sprinkle flour mixture over meringue 3 to 4 tablespoons at a time, folding in gently. Add crushed peppermint candies with the last flour addition. Spoon into an ungreased 10" tube pan. Bake at 375° 35 to 40 minutes or until top looks dry and firm. Invert to cool.

Nutritional information per serving   160 calories, 0 grams fat, 0 grams saturated fat, 0 mg cholesterol, 5 grams protein, 34 grams carbohydrate, 47 mg sodium

Variation

Chocolate-Orange Angel Food Cake. Substitute grated rind of one orange for crushed peppermint.

Fudge Cakes

Here's a rich fudgy cupcake that's great for lunch boxes.

⅔ cup brown sugar
6 tbs. cocoa
1 cup unbleached flour
1 tsp. baking soda

2 egg whites
¾ cup lowfat buttermilk
¼ cup vegetable oil
1 tsp. vanilla

In a large bowl, combine brown sugar, cocoa, flour and baking soda. In another bowl, combine egg whites, buttermilk, oil and vanilla; beat until well blended. Pour wet ingredients into dry ingredients and beat until well combined. Pour into a 12-cupcake pan sprayed with nonstick cooking spray or lined with cupcake papers. Bake at 350° for 15 to 18 minutes. Remove cupcakes from pan and cool on a wire rack.

Nutritional information per serving   139 calories, 5 grams fat, .7 grams saturated fat, 0 mg cholesterol, 3 grams protein, 21 grams carbohydrate, 96 mg sodium

Devil's Food Cake

We've thrown the fat to the devil with this one!

2 cups unbleached white flour
¾ cup brown sugar
¾ cup white sugar
½ cup cocoa
1½ tsp. baking soda

4 egg whites
1 tsp. vanilla
½ cup reduced calorie mayonnaise
1¼ cup lowfat buttermilk

In a medium bowl, combine flour and baking soda; set aside. In a mixer bowl, combine sugars, cocoa, mayonnaise, buttermilk and 2 egg whites. Beat on medium speed 2 minutes. Add flour mixture and beat until well blended. Add vanilla. In a separate bowl, beat two remaining egg whites and gently fold into batter. Pour into a 9"x13" pan sprayed with nonstick cooking spray. Bake at 350° for 25 minutes or until a cake tester comes out clean. Cool in pan.

Nutritional information per serving   172 calories, 3 grams fat, .8 grams saturated fat, 0 mg cholesterol, 4 grams protein, 32 grams carbohydrate, 87 mg sodium

Chocolate Currant Spice Cake

Servings: 20

This moist, delicious cake is loaded with flavor. Part of the secret is in the beets!

2½ cups unbleached white flour
1 tsp. baking soda
⅓ cup cocoa
1 tsp. cinnamon
½ tsp. allspice
¼ tsp. nutmeg
½ cup dried currants

1½ cups brown sugar
¾ cup lowfat buttermilk
4 egg whites
½ cup vegetable oil
1 tsp. vanilla
1 (1 lb.) can beets, drained, pureed

In a large mixing bowl, combine all dry ingredients. In another bowl, combine buttermilk, egg whites, oil, vanilla and pureed beets; mix until well blended. Add to dry ingredients and beat on medium speed 2 minutes or until well blended. Fold in currants. Pour into a 10" bundt pan which has been sprayed with nonstick cooking spray. Bake at 350° for 45 minutes or until a cake tester comes out clean. Invert on a wire rack to cool.

Nutritional information per serving   186 calories, 6 grams fat, .6 grams saturated fat, 0 mg cholesterol, 3 grams protein, 31 grams carbohydrate, 72 mg sodium

Pineapple-Chocolate Upside Down Cake

Servings: 12

An old favorite has an unusual twist that you are going to love!

1⅔ cups flour
¾ cup sugar
¼ cup cocoa
1 tsp. baking soda
1 cup water
¼ cup vegetable oil
2 egg whites

1 tsp. vinegar
1 tsp. vanilla
1½ tbs. unsalted margarine, melted
1½ tbs. hot water
⅓ cup brown sugar
6 slices canned pineapple, packed in
   juice, drained

In mixer bowl, combine flour, white sugar, cocoa, baking soda, 1 cup water, oil, egg whites, vinegar and vanilla. Beat on low speed until well blended; beat on medium speed 2 minutes. Put margarine and 1½ tbs. hot water into the bottom of a 9"x9" baking pan. Sprinkle with brown sugar and arrange pineapple slices on top. Pour batter over pineapple and bake at 350° for 35 to 40 minutes or until a cake tester comes out clean. When done, invert onto a serving plate to cool; or serve warm.

Nutritional information per serving   199 calories, 7 grams fat, .8 grams saturated fat, 0 mg cholesterol, 3 grams protein, 33 grams carbohydrate, 76 mg sodium

Easy Chocolate Cake

Servings: 16

This is Betty's famous chocolate cake. It's delicious with or without the meringue icing.

1 cup whole wheat pastry flour
1 cup unbleached white flour
1¼ cups sugar
½ cup cocoa
1 tbs. baking soda

2 egg whites
⅓ cup vegetable oil
1 cup lowfat buttermilk
1 cup boiling water

In a large bowl, sift dry ingredients; set aside. In a small bowl, combine egg whites, oil and buttermilk. Add to dry ingredients alternately with boiling water and mix well. Pour into a lightly greased 9"x13" pan. Bake at 350° for 25 to 30 minutes. Cool slightly. Spread top with meringue and bake at 400° for 5 to 8 minutes or until browned.

Meringue

2 egg whites
⅛ tsp. cream of tartar

¼ cup sugar

Whip whites with cream of tartar to soft peaks. Gradually add sugar and whip to firm peaks.

Nutritional information per serving 184 calories, 5 grams fat, 1 gram saturated fat, 0 mg cholesterol, 4 grams protein, 32 grams carbohydrate, 185 mg sodium

Anniversary Cake

Guests at Mark and Susan's anniversary party couldn't believe this delicious cake was lowfat!

¾ cup boiling water
6 tbs. cocoa
1½ tsp. baking soda
1½ tsp. vanilla
6 tbs. unsalted margarine
1½ cups sugar

6 egg whites
2¼ cups unbleached white flour
2¼ tsp. baking powder
¾ cup plain lowfat yogurt
½ cup sugarless raspberry jam

In a small bowl, combine water with cocoa and baking soda, stirring to dissolve cocoa. Cool slightly. Add vanilla and set aside. In a large bowl, cream margarine with sugar and egg whites. Stir in flour and baking powder alternately with yogurt. Stir in water mixture and mix well. Pour into 3 lightly greased 8" cake pans fitted with waxed paper circles. Bake at 350° for about 25 minutes. Cool 15 minutes and remove cake from pans to finish cooling. Place one cake layer on a serving plate. Spread with ¼ cup of jam. Add second layer and spread with remaining jam. Top with third layer. Ice top of cake and pipe a shell border around edge. Decorate with fresh flowers.

Icing

½ cup sugar
¼ cup water
2 egg whites

⅛ tsp. cream of tartar
¼ cup unsalted margarine
2 tsp. vanilla

In a small saucepan, heat sugar and water over medium heat to 238° (soft ball stage), taking care not to burn. Remove from heat. In a mixing bowl, whip egg whites with cream of tartar to soft, wet peaks. Slowly add hot syrup while continuing to whip whites. Whip until meringue is firm and cooled. In a small bowl, beat margarine and vanilla together. Add slowly to meringue. Beat until smooth.

Nutritional information per serving 199 calories, 7 grams fat, 1 gram saturated fat, 0 mg cholesterol, 3 grams protein, 32 grams carbohydrate, 109 mg sodium

Chocolate Bran Snack Cake

Enjoy this healthy snack cake often. It makes a good addition to a lunch box.

1/2 cup whole wheat pastry flour
1/2 cup unbleached white flour
3 tbs. cocoa
2 tbs. bran
3/4 tsp. baking soda
1/4 tsp. cinnamon

1/8 tsp. cloves
2 egg whites
3 tbs. vegetable oil
1/2 cup lowfat buttermilk
1/3 cup honey
1 tsp. vanilla

In a large bowl, sift dry ingredients. In another bowl, combine wet ingredients. Add to dry ingredients and mix until blended. Pour into a lightly greased 8"x8" pan. Sprinkle on topping. Bake at 350° for 25 to 30 minutes. Cool. Drizzle with glaze.

Topping

1/2 cup quick oats
2 tbs. bran
1 tbs. vegetable oil

1 tbs. honey
1/4 tsp. cinnamon

Combine all ingredients.

Glaze

¼ cup powdered sugar
1 tbs. cocoa

2 tsp. hot water

Beat together until smooth.

Nutritional information per serving   178 calories, 7 grams fat, 1 gram saturated fat, 0 mg cholesterol, 3 grams protein, 28 grams carbohydrate, 180 mg sodium

Chocolate Flan

Vary the flavor of this cake by using any fresh fruit that's in season.

1/4 cup unsalted margarine
1/3 cup sugar
2 egg whites
2 tsp. vanilla
3/4 cup unbleached white flour
1/2 cup whole wheat pastry flour

3 tbs. cocoa
1/2 tsp. baking powder
1/4 tsp. baking soda
2/3 cup lowfat buttermilk
1/4 cup sugarless raspberry jam
1 1/2 cups fresh raspberries

In a large bowl, cream margarine, sugar and one egg white. Add other white with vanilla. In another bowl, sift dry ingredients; add to creamed mixture alternately with buttermilk. Pour into a lightly greased 10" flan pan. Bake at 375° for 15 to 18 minutes. Cool in pan 10 minutes. Remove from pan, cool completely, and spread jam over top of cake. Top with raspberries.

Nutritional information per serving   129 calories, 4 grams fat, 1 gram saturated fat, 0 mg cholesterol, 2 grams protein, 21 grams carbohydrate, 58 mg sodium

Marble Chiffon Cake

Servings: 10

This cake is so light and moist it needs no icing.

3/4 cup *plus* 2 tbs. unbleached white
  flour
2/3 cups sugar
1½ tsp. baking powder
¼ cup vegetable oil
6 tbs. water

2 egg yolks
1 tsp. vanilla
½ tsp. almond extract
4 egg whites
¼ tsp. cream of tartar
1 tbs. cocoa

In a large bowl, sift flour, sugar and baking powder. In another bowl, combine next five ingredients and stir into flour mixture. In a mixer bowl, whip egg whites with cream of tartar to stiff, wet peaks. Fold whites into batter. Spoon into an ungreased 9" tube pan, leaving about ½ cup batter in bowl. Sift cocoa over reserved batter and fold in. Drop cocoa mixture onto batter in tube pan. Cut in with a knife. Bake in lower third of oven at 325° for 45 to 50 minutes. Cool upside down.

Nutritional information per serving   158 calories, 7 grams fat, 1 gram saturated fat, 50 mg cholesterol, 3 grams protein, 21 grams carbohydrate, 86 mg sodium

Hot Milk Sponge Cake

Servings: 9

This is a simple, yet elegant, cake to serve anytime.

¼ cup unsalted margarine
½ cup skim milk
3 egg whites
1 egg yolk
⅔ cup sugar

¾ cup unbleached white flour
¼ cup cocoa
½ tsp. baking soda
½ tsp. baking powder

In a small saucepan, heat margarine and milk until margarine melts. In a large bowl, whip egg whites and yolk with sugar until thick and lemon colored. In another bowl, sift dry ingredients. Carefully fold flour mixture into eggs. Lightly stir in margarine and milk. Batter will be runny. Quickly pour batter into a 9" cake pan that has been lightly greased on the bottom only and lined with waxed paper. Bake at 350° for 25 minutes. Cool upside down. Place on a serving plate. Spread white icing over cake. Use chocolate icing to make a spiral design on top.

Icing

½ cup powdered sugar
1 tbs. hot water
¼ tsp. vanilla

2 tbs. nonfat dry milk powder
½ tsp. cocoa

In a small bowl, combine all ingredients except cocoa. Beat until smooth. Remove 2 teaspoons icing, add cocoa and mix well.

Nutritional information per serving   193 calories, 6 grams fat, 1 gram saturated fat, 28 mg cholesterol, 4 grams protein, 31 grams carbohydrate, 103 mg sodium

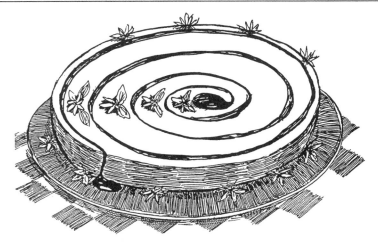

Cherry-Chocolate Torte

Servings: 10

This festive cake is perfect for any occasion.

½ cup unbleached white flour
¼ cup whole wheat pastry flour
3 tbs. cocoa
1 tsp. baking powder
½ tsp. baking soda

2 egg yolks
⅔ cup sugar, divided
¼ cup hot water
2 egg whites

In a small bowl, sift together first five ingredients. Set aside. In a large bowl, whip yolks, gradually adding ⅓ cup sugar. Add water a tablespoon at a time and whip until light and lemon colored. Set aside. In another bowl, whip whites to soft peaks. Gradually add remaining sugar and whip to firm peaks. Fold flour mixture into yolks, and then fold in whites. Pour into a 9" springform pan that has been greased on the bottom only and lined with waxed paper. Bake at 350° for 25 minutes. Cool upside down. Freeze cake for easier cutting. Slice frozen cake in half horizontally. Place bottom half on a serving plate and cover with half the cherry filling. Top with other half of cake and spread remaining cherry filling over top. Pipe a shell border around top and bottom of cake.

Cherry Filling

2 cups sour pie cherries thawed,
  drained, 1/3 cup juice reserved
3 tbs. sugar

2 tbs. cornstarch
1/8 tsp. almond extract

Heat cherries and sugar. Combine cornstarch and juice. Stir into hot cherries and cook until thickened and clear. Remove from heat and add almond extract.

Icing

1/4 cup nonfat dry milk powder
1/4 cup ice water
1 tsp. lemon juice

3 tbs. sugar
1/4 cup unsalted margarine
1 tsp. vanilla

In a medium bowl, whip milk with water to firm peaks, gradually adding lemon juice and sugar. In another bowl, whip margarine; add with vanilla to milk mixture.

Nutritional information per serving   198 calories, 6 grams fat, 1 gram saturated fat, 50 mg cholesterol, 4 grams protein, 35 grams carbohydrate, 113 mg sodium

Raspberry-Filled Chocolate Cupcakes

Servings: 9

There's a surprise filling in these chocolate-iced cupcakes.

1/4 cup boiling water
2 tbs. cocoa
1/2 tsp. baking soda
1/2 tsp. vanilla
2 tbs. unsalted margarine
1/2 cup sugar

2 egg whites
3/4 cup unbleached white flour
3/4 tsp. baking powder
1/4 cup plain lowfat yogurt
1/4 cup sugarless raspberry jam

In a small bowl, combine water with cocoa and baking soda, stirring to dissolve cocoa. Cool slightly, add vanilla and set aside. In a large bowl, cream margarine with sugar and egg whites. Stir in flour and baking powder alternately with yogurt. Stir in water mixture and mix well. Spoon into 9 cupcake tins lined with foil liners. Bake at 350° for 20 to 22 minutes. Cool. Spoon jam into a pastry bag fitted with a plain tip. Poke a small hole in top of each cupcake with a knife. Pipe jam into holes and ice.

Icing

2/3 cup powdered sugar
2 tbs. cocoa

1 tbs. Neufchatel cheese
1 tbs. skim milk

In a medium bowl, cream all ingredients together.

Nutritional information per serving 173 calories, 2 grams fat, 1 gram saturated fat, 1 mg cholesterol, 3 grams protein, 32 grams carbohydrate, 79 mg sodium

Sweetheart Cake

Make a lowfat valentine for the ones you love.

1 cup unbleached white flour
¾ tsp. baking powder
¼ tsp. baking soda
¼ cup cocoa
¼ cup unsalted margarine

½ cup brown sugar
½ tsp. vanilla
¾ cup skim milk
2 egg whites

In a medium bowl, sift flour, baking powder, baking soda and cocoa. Set aside. In a large bowl, cream margarine with brown sugar and vanilla. Add flour mixture alternately with milk. Whip egg whites to firm, wet peaks and fold into batter. Lightly grease an 8" heart-shaped pan and line bottom with waxed paper cut to fit. Pour batter into pan and bake at 350° for 25 minutes. Cool in pan for 15 minutes; remove from pan to finish cooling. Ice cake with fluffy icing and decorate with fresh flowers.

Fluffy Icing

½ cup water
⅓ cup sugar
⅛ tsp. cream of tartar
2 egg whites, room temperature
drop of red food color or 2 tbs. cocoa (optional)

In a saucepan, boil water and sugar to 238° (soft ball stage). Remove from heat. In a medium bowl, whip egg whites with cream of tartar to soft peaks. Slowly pour in hot syrup and whip to firm peaks. Add food color, if desired, or sift in cocoa.

Nutritional information per serving 199 calories, 6 grams fat, 1 gram saturated fat, 0 mg cholesterol, 5 grams protein, 33 grams carbohydrate, 66 mg sodium

Double Mint Cake

A double dose of mint, in both the cake and icing, combined with a complementary chocolate glaze, is a delicious way to satisfy your chocolate cravings.

1 cup unbleached white flour
¾ cup whole wheat pastry flour
1 tsp. baking soda
½ tsp. baking powder
1 cup sugar

2 tbs. unsalted margarine
3 tbs. cocoa
2 egg whites
½ tsp. peppermint extract
1 cup lowfat buttermilk

In a medium bowl, sift flours, baking soda and baking powder; set aside. In a large bowl, cream sugar, margarine, cocoa and egg whites. Stir in peppermint extract. Add flour mixture alternately with buttermilk and mix well. Pour into two lightly greased 8" cake pans fitted with waxed paper linings. Bake at 350° for about 25 minutes. Cool for 15 minutes in pans and remove to finish cooling. Place one cake layer on a serving plate. Spread with a thin layer of mint icing and top with a thin layer of chocolate glaze. Place second layer on top of first and repeat.

Mint Icing

1 cup powdered sugar
1 oz. Neufchatel cheese

1 tbs. skim milk
½ tsp. mint extract

In a small bowl, cream ingredients until well blended.

Chocolate Glaze

3 tbs. cocoa
½ cup sugar
2 tbs. cornstarch

½ cup boiling water
½ tbs. unsalted margarine
1 tsp. vanilla

In a saucepan, combine cocoa, sugar and cornstarch. Whisk in boiling water slowly. Cook until thickened. Remove from heat; add margarine and vanilla. Cool before using.

Nutritional information per serving 192 calories, 3 grams fat, 1 gram saturated fat, 2 mg cholesterol, 3 grams protein, 39 grams carbohydrate, 186 mg sodium

Glazed Chocolate Almond Loaf

Servings: 12

The applesauce adds moisture, but not fat, to this light version of chocolate pound cake.

¾ cup whole wheat pastry flour
1 cup unbleached white flour
⅓ cup cocoa
1 tsp. baking soda
1 cup unsweetened applesauce
¼ cup vegetable oil

⅓ cup brown sugar, lightly packed
2 egg whites
2 tbs. chopped almonds
2 tbs. sugarless apricot jam, heated, strained
slivered almonds

In a medium bowl, sift flours, cocoa, baking powder and baking soda. Set aside. In a large bowl, combine applesauce, oil, brown sugar and egg whites. Beat well until sugar is dissolved. Stir in flour mixture. Spoon into a lightly greased 4"x8" loaf pan. Bake at 350° for 40 to 45 minutes. Glaze with jam while still warm. Place slivered almonds on loaf in a pleasing design.

Nutritional information per serving 164 calories, 6 grams fat, 1 gram saturated fat, 0 mg cholesterol, 4 grams protein, 24 grams carbohydrate, 81 mg sodium

Pies and Tarts

The pie crust recipes are together at the beginning of this chapter. When a recipe calls for a particular crust, refer to this section to find it before proceeding with the recipe.

Because the crusts have a minimal amount of fat, it's a good idea to spray the pan lightly with a nonstick cooking spray before the crust is placed in it. Always use chilled margarine and ice water for a pastry crust.

One of the easiest ways to roll out a crust is by using waxed paper. Dampen your work surface and lay out a sheet of waxed paper. The moisture keeps the paper from moving. Put the dough in the middle of the paper and, if desired, top with a second sheet of waxed paper. Some may find it easier not to use the second sheet. (If you don't use it, lightly flour the top of the dough before rolling it out.) When the dough is rolled slightly larger than the pan, remove the top paper and gently flip the dough into the pan. Carefully remove the bottom paper. Experiment to see which method is easier for you.

Crusts

Basic Crust #1

½ cup whole wheat pastry flour
½ cup unbleached white flour
½ tsp. baking powder

3 tbs. unsalted margarine
2-3 tbs. ice water

In a medium bowl, sift dry ingredients. Cut in margarine. Add enough ice water to hold dough together. Roll out on a floured surface. Place in a 9" pie pan and prick crust all over with a fork. Bake at 375° for 10 minutes until light brown. Cool before filling.

Basic Crust #2

½ cup whole wheat pastry flour
½ cup unbleached white flour
1 tbs. sugar

3 tbs. unsalted margarine
3-4 tbs. ice water

In a medium bowl, combine flours and sugar. Cut in margarine. Add enough ice water to hold dough together. Roll out on a floured surface. Place in a 10" tart pan with a removable bottom and prick crust all over with a fork. Bake at 375° for 7 minutes until light brown. Cool before filling.

Graham Cracker Crust #1

1 tbs. unsalted margarine
2 tbs. orange juice concentrate

¾ cup graham cracker crumbs

In a saucepan, melt margarine and juice concentrate. Stir thoroughly with crumbs. Press into a 9" pie pan. Bake at 375° for 7 minutes. Cool before filling.

Graham Cracker Crust #2

1 tbs. unsalted margarine
2 tbs. orange juice concentrate

¾ cup graham cracker crumbs
2 tbs. cocoa

In a saucepan, melt margarine and juice concentrate. In a medium bowl, combine cocoa and crumbs. Pour liquids into crumb mixture and combine thoroughly. Bake at 375° for 7 minutes. Cool before filling.

Meringue Crust #1

3 egg whites
¼ cup sugar

½ tsp. cream of tartar
¼ tsp. vanilla

In a mixer bowl, beat egg whites until foamy. Add cream of tartar and beat on high speed, adding sugar one tablespoon at a time until stiff, glossy peaks form. Spread in a pie plate to form a crust. Bake at 200° for 4 hours or until thoroughly dry. Cool and store in an airtight container.

Meringue Crust #2

Add 2 tbs. cocoa to sugar before beating with egg whites.

Meringue Crust #3

Add ¼ tsp. almond extract to egg whites during beating. Gently fold in ⅓ cup coarsely ground almonds after beating egg whites.

Filo Fruit Cups

Use these versatile cups for any fruit fillings.

Filo Cups
4 sheets filo dough
1 tbs. unsalted margarine, melted

Place one sheet of filo on work surface, keeping others covered. Lightly brush sheet with margarine. Place a second sheet on top. Brush again. Cut into thirds, lengthwise. Stack strips together. Cut into four equal sections. Press each section into a light greased muffin tin. Prick bottoms with a fork. Repeat procedure with remaining two sheets of filo. Bake at 375° for 10 minutes, or until golden. Remove from tins and cool. Spoon ¼ cup filling into each cup. Pour 1 tbs. chocolate sauce over filling.

Filling
4 cups fresh raspberries

In a saucepan, bring 2 cups raspberries to a boil. Remove from heat. Crush slightly. Stir in remaining raspberries.

Chocolate Sauce

2 tbs. cocoa
1/4 cup sugar
2 tsp. cornstarch

1/2 cup water
1/2 tsp. unsalted margarine
1/2 tsp. vanilla

In a saucepan, combine dry ingredients. Add water and cook until thickened. Remove from heat; stir in margarine and vanilla. Serve warm.

Nutritional information per serving   101 calories, 3 grams fat, 0 grams saturated fat, 0 mg cholesterol, 2 grams protein, 18 grams carbohydrate, 61 mg sodium

Cheesy Chocolate Pie

Servings: 8

This pie is quick and easy to prepare.

Graham Cracker Crust #2, page 91
1 envelope plain gelatin
¼ cup water
4 ozs. neufchatel cheese, room
  temperature
1 cup skim milk

¼ cup cocoa
½ cup powdered sugar
1 tsp. vanilla
1 egg white
1 tbs. sugar

   In a saucepan, soften gelatin in water. Heat to dissolve. In a food processor, blend cheese, milk, cocoa, powdered sugar and vanilla. Add gelatin and blend. In a mixer bowl, mix egg white to soft peaks. Add sugar slowly and whip to firm peaks. Fold into mixture and pour in prepared crust. Chill several hours until set.

Nutritional information per serving   163 calories, 6 grams fat, 3 grams saturated fat, 11 mg cholesterol, 6 grams protein, 22 grams carbohydrate, 118 mg sodium

Choco-Mint Freezer Pie

Cool mint ice "cream" is sandwiched between chocolate layers.

Graham Cracker Crust #2, page 91

2½ cups lowfat vanilla ice milk, softened

¼ tsp. mint extract

In a medium bowl, stir mint extract into ice milk. Pour ⅓ hot chocolate sauce into prepared crust. Spread over bottom. Freeze 20 minutes to set. Carefully spoon ice milk over chocolate bottom. Smooth top with a spatula. Freeze until firm. Spread remaining cooled chocolate sauce over top. Freeze to set sauce.

Chocolate Sauce

2 tbs. cocoa
¼ cup sugar
2 tsp. cornstarch

½ cup water
½ tsp. unsalted margarine
1 tsp. vanilla

In a saucepan, combine dry ingredients. Add water and cook until thickened. Remove from heat and stir in margarine and vanilla.

Nutritional information per serving 167 calories, 5 grams fat, 1 gram saturated fat, 0 mg cholesterol, 3 grams protein, 29 grams carbohydrate, 71 mg sodium

Chocolate Chiffon Pie

Servings: 8

This pie will tempt you with mounds of fluffy, light chocolate filling in a graham cracker crust.

Graham Cracker Crust #1, page 90
1 envelope plain gelatin
1/4 cup sugar
1/3 cup cocoa
1/3 cup water
1 cup evaporated skim milk

1 egg yolk
3 egg whites
1/4 tsp. cream of tartar
1/3 cup sugar
1/2 cup evaporated skim milk, frozen
  until ice forms on sides

In a saucepan, combine gelatin, sugar, cocoa and water. Let gelatin soften for 5 minutes. Stir in 1 cup evaporated skim milk. Bring to a boil, stirring. Add egg yolk and return to boil. Place in a bowl and chill until mixture mounds in a spoon. In a mixer bowl, whip whites with cream of tartar to soft peaks. Slowly add 1/3 cup sugar and whip to firm peaks. In another bowl, whip iced evaporated skim milk to firm peaks. Fold whites into custard mixture; fold in whipped milk. Spoon into crust and chill several hours before serving.

Nutritional information per serving   186 calories, 4 grams fat, 1 gram saturated fat, 33 mg cholesterol, 8 grams protein, 31 grams carbohydrate, 114 mg sodium

Tin Roof Pie

Servings: 8

Peanuts and chocolate are combined in a lucious frozen ice "cream" pie.

Graham Cracker Crust #1, page 90
3 cups lowfat vanilla ice milk, softened

¼ cup plain unsalted peanuts, chopped

In a medium bowl, stir peanuts into ice milk. Swirl chocolate sauce into ice milk. Spoon into crust and freeze until firm.

Chocolate Sauce

2 tbs. cocoa
¼ cup sugar
2 tsp. cornstarch

½ cup water
½ tsp. unsalted margarine
½ tsp. vanilla

In a saucepan, combine dry ingredients. Add water and cook until thickened. Remove from heat and stir in margarine and vanilla. Cool slightly.

Nutritional information per serving   174 calories, 7 grams fat, 2 grams saturated fat, 7 mg cholesterol, 4 grams protein, 25 grams carbohydrate, 77 mg sodium

Tropical Fudge-Bottom Pie

We've developed a light, fruity version of this popular pie.

Graham Cracker Crust #1, page 90
1/3 cup sugar
1/4 cup cornstarch
2 cups skim milk
1 egg yolk
1 tbs. cocoa
1 (8 ozs.) can unsweetened crushed
  pineapple, drained, 1/4 cup juice
  reserved

2 tsp. plain gelatin
2 tbs. orange juice concentrate
1 large banana
2 egg whites
1/8 tsp. cream of tartar
2 tbs. sugar

In a saucepan, combine sugar, cornstarch, milk and egg yolk. Cook over medium heat, stirring, until thickened. Place in a bowl and set aside. Transfer 1 cup of filling to a large bowl. Add sifted cocoa, stirring to blend, and pour into prepared pie crust. Chill. In a small saucepan, soften gelatin in pineapple juice. Add orange juice and heat to dissolve. Stir into remaining filling and chill until mixture begins to set. In a mixer bowl, whip whites with cream of tartar to soft peaks. Slowly add sugar and whip to firm peaks. Fold into chilled filling.

Slice banana over chocolate bottom in crust. Spoon filling on top. Chill several hours. Before serving, spoon crushed pineapple around edges of pie.

Nutritional information per serving 192 calories, 4 grams fat, 1 gram saturated fat, 32 mg cholesterol, 5 grams protein, 36 grams carbohydrate, 84 mg sodium

Chocolate Meringue Pie

Servings: 9

It's hard to believe that this old favorite is also good for you. If you don't spread meringue to the edge, so that it touches the crust, it will shrink away from the sides when you brown it, and become an island!

Basic Crust #1, page 90
⅓ cup cocoa
⅓ cup nonfat dry milk powder
¼ cup sugar

¼ cup cornstarch
2½ cups skim milk
½ tbs. unsalted margarine
2 tsp. vanilla

In a small bowl, combine cocoa, milk powder and sugar. In a cup, mix cornstarch with ½ cup skim milk. Pour remaining skim milk into a saucepan, whisk in dry ingredients and bring to a boil over medium heat. Slowly add cornstarch mixture, stirring constantly. Cook until thickened. Remove from heat and add margarine and vanilla. Pour into prepared pie crust. Top with meringue, making sure to cover edges of pie. Bake at 400° for 6 to 8 minutes until meringue is light brown. Cool before serving.

Meringue

3 egg whites
1/4 tsp. cream of tartar

3 tbs. sugar

In a mixer bowl, whip whites with cream of tartar to soft peaks. Slowly add sugar and whip to firm peaks.

Nutritional information per serving 195 calories, 5 grams fat, 1 gram saturated fat, 1 mg cholesterol, 8 grams protein, 30 grams carbohydrate, 120 mg sodium

Cherry Chocolate Cream Tart

Servings: 12

This tart has a creamy, chocolate cheese layer covered with a cherry topping.

Basic Crust #2, page 90
6 ozs. neufchatel cheese, room
  temperature
1/3 cup sugar
2 tbs. skim milk

2 tbs. cocoa
1 tbs. unbleached white flour
2 egg whites
1/4 tsp. almond extract

In a medium bowl, beat all together until smooth and creamy. Pour into crust. Bake at 350° for 20 minutes. Remove from oven and spread cherry topping over filling. Return to oven and bake 12 to 15 minutes more until set.

Cherry Topping

2 cups sour cherries
2 tbs. honey

2 tbs. cherry juice
1 tbs. cornstarch

In a saucepan, heat cherries and honey. Dissolve cornstarch in juice and stir into cherries; cook until thickened and clear. Cool slightly before using.

Nutritional information per serving   153 calories, 6 grams fat, 3 grams saturated fat, 11 mg cholesterol, 4 grams protein, 21 grams carbohydrate, 68 mg sodium

Chocolate-Peanut Butter Ice Cream Pie   Servings: 10

This sounds sinfully rich, but it isn't. It's also quick and easy.

Graham Cracker Crust #1, page 90, baked in a 10" pie plate

6 cups chocolate lowfat ice milk
3 tbs. peanut butter, no sugar added

Soften ice milk and put it in a bowl, Gently swirl in peanut butter. Pile mixture into crust. Cover with plastic wrap and freeze 6 hours or overnight.

Nutritional information per serving   185 calories, 7 grams fat, 3 grams saturated fat, 11 mg cholesterol, 5 grams protein, 26 grams carbohydrate, 235 mg sodium

Chocolate Custard Yogurt Pie

Servings: 9

This rich, satisfying dessert will put a temporary end to chocolate cravings.

1 Basic Crust #1, page 90,
 baked for 5 minutes
2 tbs. flour
½ cup *plus* 1 tbs. sugar
¼ cup cocoa

1 egg *plus* 3 egg whites
2 cups plain lowfat yogurt
2 tsp. vanilla
fresh fruit (optional)

In a small bowl, mix flour, sugar and cocoa; set aside. In a mixing bowl, beat egg and egg whites, yogurt and vanilla on medium speed 1 minute. Add dry ingredients and blend well. Pour into pie shell and bake at 350° 1 hour or until center appears set. Remove from oven and cool on a wire rack. Garnish each serving with fresh fruit, if desired.

Nutritional information per serving 198 calories, 6 grams fat, 1.6 grams saturated fat, 27 mg cholesterol, 7 grams protein, 31 grams carbohydrate, 56 mg sodium

Brown and White Custard Pie

Servings: 9

This is the perfect light and luscious end to a meal.

Meringue Crust #2, page 91
1/3 cup sugar
1/4 cup cornstarch
1 egg

2 cups skim milk
1 tbs. margarine
2 tsp. vanilla
1-2 tsp. cocoa

In a heavy-bottomed saucepan, mix sugar and cornstarch. Beat egg and milk together and add slowly to sugar-cornstarch mixture. Heat, stirring constantly until mixture boils; boil for 1 minute. Remove from heat and add margarine and vanilla; stir until well blended. Transfer custard to a bowl and cover the surface with plastic wrap. Cool to room temperature. When custard is cool, beat briefly with a hand or electric mixer and spoon into meringue shell. Dust top with 1 or 2 teaspoons of cocoa through a tea strainer.

Nutritional information per serving   113 calories, 2 grams fat, .6 grams saturated fat, 28 mg cholesterol, 4 grams protein, 19 grams carbohydrate, 51 mg sodium

Chocolate Cheese Tarts

Servings: 8

These tarts are little gems!

Basic Crust #1, page 90, rolled out,
  unbaked
1 (16 oz.) carton lowfat ricotta cheese
2 tbs. cocoa

4 tbs. sugar
1 tsp. vanilla
sliced fresh fruit of your choice
¼ cup low sugar apricot jam

Line eight 4" tart pans with pie crust dough. Prick bottoms with a fork, place on a cookie sheet and bake at 450° for 8 to 10 minutes. Cool. In a food processor or mixer bowl, combine ricotta, cocoa, sugar and vanilla. Blend until very smooth and creamy. Spread 3 tbs. of mixture in each tart shell. Arrange sliced fruit decoratively on top. Melt jam in a small saucepan over low heat, or in a microwave. Spoon jam over fruit to glaze. Chill several hours before serving.

Nutritional information per serving 196 calories, 8 grams protein, 29 grams carbohydrate, 7 grams total fat, 1 gram saturated fat, 0 mg cholesterol, 77 mg sodium

Chocolate Banana Cream Tarts

Servings: 9

Basic Crust #1, rolled out, unbaked
1/3 cup sugar
2 tbs. cornstarch
1 egg

2 cups skim milk
1 tsp. vanilla
1/2 banana, mashed
1 banana, sliced

Line nine 4" tart pans with pie crust dough. Prick bottoms with a fork, place on a cookie sheet and bake at 450° for 8 to 10 minutes. Cool. In a saucepan, combine sugar and cornstarch. Beat egg and milk together and add slowly to sugar-cornstarch mixture. Heat, stirring constantly until mixture boils; boil 1 minute. Remove from heat and stir in vanilla and mashed banana. Cool covered with plastic wrap. Pour into tart shells, arrange sliced bananas on top and drizzle 2 tsp. chocolate sauce over each tart. Serve at once.

Chocolate Sauce

1 tbs. margarine
2 1/2 tsp. cocoa

2 tbs. powdered sugar
2 1/2 tsp. skim milk

In a small saucepan, melt margarine and add cocoa, powdered sugar and milk. Stir until well blended and cocoa and sugar have dissolved.

Nutritional information per serving   188 calories, 6 grams fat, 1 gram saturated fat, 28 mg cholesterol, 4 grams protein, 29 grams carbohydrate, 25 mg sodium

Black-Bottom Pumpkin Chiffon Pie

Servings: 9

Chocolate offers a new twist to a traditional favorite.

Graham Cracker Crust #1, page 90

Chocolate Layer

3 tbs. sugar
3 tbs. cocoa
1 tbs. cornstarch

1 cup skim milk
½ tsp. vanilla

In a saucepan, combine sugar, cocoa and cornstarch. Gradually add milk and cook over medium heat until mixture comes to a boil; boil 1 minute. Remove from heat and stir in vanilla. Cool slightly. Spread in the bottom of crust and set aside.

Pumpkin Layer

1 pkg. gelatin
¼ cup cold water
1 (16 ozs.) can pumpkin
1 egg *plus* 2 egg whites
½ cup evaporated skim milk
⅓ cup sugar

¾ tsp. *each* cinnamon, ginger, nutmeg
¼ tsp. allspice
3 egg whites
¼ tsp. cream of tartar
3 tbs. sugar

Dissolve gelatin in ¼ cup cold water and set aside. In a heavy-bottomed saucepan, combine pumpkin, beaten egg and 2 egg whites, evaporated milk, ⅓ cup sugar and spices. Cook over low heat until thickened, about 10 minutes, stirring constantly. Add gelatin mixture and stir until gelatin is dissolved. Remove from heat and cool to room temperature. In a mixer bowl, beat remaining egg whites until foamy; add cream of tartar. Continue beating on high speed, adding sugar 1 tablespoon at a time, until stiff, glossy peaks form. Beat ½ cup of the egg whites into the cooled pumpkin mixture. Pour pumpkin mixture over beaten egg whites and gently fold together. Pour into chocolate-lined crust and chill 6 hours or overnight.

Nutritional information per serving   183 calories, 3 grams fat, 1 gram saturated fat, 28 mg cholesterol, 7 grams protein, 33 grams carbohydrate, 243 mg sodium

Fudge-Bottom Pie

Servings: 8

We've scaled down the fat, but not the taste.

Graham Cracker Crust #2, page 91

Chocolate Layer

3 tbs. cocoa
3 tbs. sugar
1 tbs. cornstarch

1 cup skim milk
½ tsp margarine
½ tsp. vanilla

In a saucepan, mix cocoa, sugar and cornstarch. Add milk slowly, stirring until well blended. Boil and stir 1 minute, remove from heat; stir in margarine and vanilla. Cool slightly and pour into prepared pie crust. Chill.

Vanilla Layer

⅓ cup sugar
¼ cup cornstarch
2 cups skim milk

1 egg
1 tbs. margarine
1 tsp. vanilla

In a saucepan, mix sugar and cornstarch. Beat egg together with milk; gradually add to sugar-cornstarch mixture, stirring until well blended. Coover over medium heat until mixture boils. Boil and stir 1 minute. Remove from heat and add margarine and vanilla. Cool slightly and pour over chocolate layer. Cover surface with plastic wrap and chill when filling has cooled to room temperature.

Nutritional information per serving 199 calories, 6 grams fat, 1.5 grams saturated fat, 33 mg cholesterol, 5 grams protein, 33 grams carbohydrate, 233 mg sodium

Mocha Almond Ice Cream Pie

Servings: 8

This is an elegant dessert to offer guests. Remember to keep the meringue in an air-tight container until ready to serve.

Meringue Crust #3, page 91
1½ tbs. cocoa
⅓ cup powdered sugar
1 tbs. skim milk

1 tsp. instant coffee dissolved in 1 tsp. hot water
6 cups lowfat vanilla ice milk

In a small saucepan, mix cocoa, powdered sugar, milk and dissolved instant coffee. Stir over medium heat just until well blended. Cool. Let ice milk soften in a large bowl. Drizzle mocha sauce over ice milk and stir until mixture is swirled throughout. Pile ice milk into a pie plate or shallow bowl with a smaller diameter than the inside of the meringue crust. (The refrozen ice milk must fit into the crust.) Cover surface of ice milk with plastic wrap and freeze 6 hours or overnight. Unwrap ice milk and fit into crust just before serving. Use a knife dipped in hot water to cut.

Nutritional information per serving   187 calories, 4 grams fat, 2 grams saturated fat, 13 mg cholesterol, 6 grams protein, 32 grams carbohydrate, 86 mg sodium

Chocolate Peanut Butter Swirl Pie

Servings: 9

This one is for kids and peanut butter lovers of all ages.

Graham Cracker Crust #1, page 90
⅓ cup sugar
¼ cup cornstarch
6 tbs. cocoa

1 egg
2 cups skim milk
1 tsp. vanilla
2 tbs. peanut butter

In a heavy-bottomed saucepan, mix sugar, cornstarch and cocoa. Beat egg and milk together and slowly add to sugar mixture, stirring constantly. Cook over medium heat until mixture boils and thickens. Boil 1 minute. Remove from heat and stir in vanilla; add peanut butter and swirl. Pour into crust. Chill several hours before serving.

Nutritional information per serving 159 calories, 5 grams fat, 1 gram saturated fat, 28 mg cholesterol, 5 grams protein, 24 grams carbohydrate, 204 mg sodium

Fudge-Dipped Strawberry Tart

Servings: 12

This dessert makes a beautiful presentation. You will impress the guests with your genius even before they find out how low in fat it is.

Basic Crust #1, page 90, rolled out, unbaked
1/3 cup sugar
1/4 cup cornstarch
2 cups skim milk

1 egg
1 tbs. margarine
2 tsp. vanilla or 1 tsp. almond extract
2 cups ripe strawberries of uniform size

Prepare pastry and fit dough into an 8"x12" flan pan. Prick bottom and sides and bake at 450° for 10 to 12 minutes. Cool. In a heavy-bottomed saucepan, mix sugar and cornstarch. Beat milk and egg together and slowly add to sugar mixture. Heat over medium heat, stirring constantly, until mixture boils. Boil and stir 1 minute. Remove from heat and stir in margarine and flavoring. Spread in cooled flan crust; cool. Prepare fudge sauce. Wash, dry and cut the stem end from each strawberry. Dip tip of each strawberry into Fudge Sauce and arrange in rows on top of flan. Chill several hours before serving.

Fudge Sauce

2 tbs. margarine
1 tbs. *plus* 1 tsp. cocoa

¼ cup powdered sugar
1 tbs. skim milk

In a small saucepan, melt margarine. Stir in cocoa, powdered sugar and milk. Heat and stir to combine well.

Nutritional information per serving   162 calories, 6.6 grams fat, 1 gram saturated fat, 22 mg cholesterol, 3 grams protein, 23 grams carbohydrate, 19 mg sodium

Desserts

A good way to help with portion control is to make desserts in single serving sizes. Not only can it be more festive and attractive, but a smaller portion can actually seem larger. A beautiful presentation creates the feeling of something special. Bring out your prettiest dessert bowls or company plates. Try adding a visual touch using garnishes. Nothing elaborate, maybe a few perfect berries in season, a fresh cut flower from the flower garden. How about a lighted candle on each serving for an unexpected surprise? Use your imagination and you can come up with endless ideas.

Party desserts are always a last minute rush to present and serve. If there's room in the refrigerator, make individual servings and garnish ahead of time. When you're ready to serve dessert, whisk them to the table without any bother, and enjoy the finale with your guests.

Chocolate Mocha Sponge

Servings: 4

Coffee lovers will enjoy the intense mocha flavor of this dessert.

1 tsp. plain gelatin
¼ cup sugar
1½ tsp. instant coffee
2 tsp. cocoa
¾ cup boiling water
1 tsp. vanilla
1 egg white

In a saucepan, combine dry ingredients. Whisk in boiling water to dissolve gelatin and coffee. Chill until set around edges. Add egg white and whip until mixture begins to hold shape, about 5 minutes. Spoon into 4 dessert glasses and chill until set.

Nutritional information per serving 57 calories, 0 grams fat, 0 grams saturated fat, 0 mg cholesterol, 2 grams protein, 13 grams carbohydrate, 13 mg sodium

Chocolate Bavarian Cream

Servings: 8

This delicious recipe proves you can make a rich, chocolatey dessert without using ingredients loaded with fat.

1 tsp. plain gelatin
1½ cups skim milk
¼ cup sugar
¼ cup cocoa
1 tsp. vanilla

2 egg whites
¼ cup sugar
⅔ cup evaporated skim milk, frozen
   until ice forms at edges

Soften gelatin in ½ cup skim milk. In a saucepan, mix sugar and cocoa. Stir in 1 cup skim milk. Heat to a boil. Stir in softened gelatin until dissolved. Remove from heat, add vanilla and chill to egg white consistency. Whip egg whites to soft peaks. Gradually add sugar and whip to firm peaks. Whip iced evaporated milk to firm peaks. Stir ¼ whites and ¼ whipped milk into chilled gelatin mixture. Carefully fold in remaining whites and milk. Spoon into a 6-cup mold. Chill until set.

Nutritional information per serving 99 calories, 1 gram fat, 0 grams saturated fat, 1 mg cholesterol, 6 grams protein, 18 grams carbohydrate, 62 mg sodium

Chocolate Tapioca

This popular old-fashioned pudding takes on a new taste with the addition of cocoa.

1½ cups skim milk
¼ cup sugar
2 tbs. cocoa
2 tbs. quick-cooking tapioca
½ tsp. vanilla
1 egg white

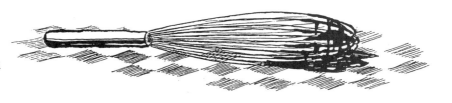

In a saucepan, combine milk, sugar, cocoa and tapioca. Let stand 5 minutes. Bring to a boil and cook over medium heat 5 to 8 minutes, until thickened. Remove from heat and add vanilla. Whip egg white to firm, wet peaks. Fold into tapioca. Spoon into 4 dessert dishes. Serve warm or chilled.

Nutritional information per serving 112 calories, 1 gram fat, 0 grams saturated fat, 1 mg cholesterol, 5 grams protein, 22 grams carbohydrate, 60 mg sodium

Chocolate Cloud Parfaits

Servings: 6

Creamy, cool chocolate is layered with fresh strawberries. This dessert is as appealing to the eye as it is to the palate.

1/2 tsp. plain gelatin
2 tbs. cold water
1/2 cup sugar
1/4 cup water
2 tbs. cocoa
1 tbs. corn syrup

1 tsp. vanilla
2 egg whites
1/2 cup evaporated skim milk, frozen
  until ice forms at edges
1 cup sliced strawberries

Soften gelatin in 2 tbs. cold water. Set aside. In a saucepan, mix sugar, water, cocoa and corn syrup. Heat over medium heat to 238° (soft ball stage). *Don't burn!* Remove from heat and stir in softened gelatin until dissolved. Add vanilla. In a mixer bowl, whip egg whites to soft peaks, slowly pouring in syrup; whip 5 minutes. In another bowl, whip iced evaporated milk to firm peaks. Fold into egg white mixture. Spoon into a container, cover and freeze several hours. To serve, thaw slightly and layer mixture with strawberries in parfait glasses.

Nutritional information per serving   104 calories, 0 grams fat, 0 grams saturated fat, 0 mg cholesterol, 4 grams protein, 22 grams carbohydrate, 46 mg sodium

Fudgy Puddin'

Servings: 4

This dense, rich pudding is a dessert the kids will love. Easy to make, too!

1 envelope plain gelatin
½ cup skim milk
¼ cup sugar
¼ cup cocoa
½ cup skim milk
1½ tsp. vanilla
½ cup ice water

In a saucepan, soften gelatin in ½ cup skim milk for 5 minutes; then heat to dissolve gelatin. In a blender, process sugar, cocoa, ½ cup milk and vanilla until smooth. Blend in gelatin mixture and add ice water. Pour into 4 dessert glasses and chill until set.

Nutritional information per serving 97 calories, 1 gram fat, 0 grams saturated fat, 1 mg cholesterol, 5 grams protein, 18 grams carbohydrate, 35 mg sodium

Almond Cream with Chocolate Sauce

Servings: 4

Delicate almond-flavored custard is served with a velvet smooth chocolate sauce.

1 envelope plain gelatin
1/4 cup water
1 1/2 cups skim milk
1/3 cup sugar

1/2 tsp. almond extract
1/2 tsp. vanilla
3/4 cup plain lowfat yogurt

Soften gelatin in water 5 minutes. In a saucepan, heat milk and sugar to a boil. Stir in gelatin to dissolve. Remove from heat, add extracts and chill until mixture begins to set. Fold in yogurt. Spoon into 4 dessert dishes and top with chocolate sauce.

Chocolate Sauce

2 tbs. cocoa
1/4 cup sugar
1/2 tbs. cornstarch

1/2 cup water
1 tsp. unsalted margarine
1 tsp. vanilla

In a saucepan, combine cocoa, sugar, cornstarch and water. Cook over medium heat until slightly thickened. Remove from heat and stir in margarine and vanilla.

Nutritional information per serving   193 calories, 2 grams fat, 0 grams saturated fat, 2 mg cholesterol, 8 grams protein, 38 grams carbohydrate, 82 mg sodium

Chocolate Sundaes

Nothing beats a bowl of ice cream smothered in chocolate sauce. Try this lowfat version next time you get the urge.

2 cups lowfat ice milk

Scoop ½ cup ice milk per dessert dish. Spoon 2 tablespoons sauce over ice milk.

Chocolate Syrup

2 tbs. cocoa
2 tbs. sugar
1 tbs. corn syrup

½ cup *plus* 2 tbs. evaporated skim milk
1 tsp. unsalted margarine
1 tsp. vanilla

In a saucepan, combine cocoa, sugar, corn syrup and milk. Bring to a boil over medium heat, stirring constantly. Boil gently 2 minutes. Remove from heat. Add margarine and vanilla.

Nutritional information per serving 175 calories, 4 grams fat, 2 grams saturated fat, 10 mg cholesterol, 6 grams protein, 29 grams carbohydrate, 104 mg sodium

Chocolate "Ice Cream"

Servings: 8

It's easy and fun to make your own ice milk at home. The recipes that follow are so delicious you won't believe they're not ice cream. Be sure to "cure" them in the freezer several hours before serving.

1 cup sugar
⅓ cup cocoa
2 cups skim milk
2 cups lowfat buttermilk
1 tsp. vanilla

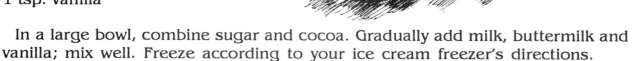

In a large bowl, combine sugar and cocoa. Gradually add milk, buttermilk and vanilla; mix well. Freeze according to your ice cream freezer's directions.

Nutritional information per serving   155 calories, 1 gram fat, .6 grams saturated fat, 3 mg cholesterol, 5 grams protein, 32 grams carbohydrate, 99 mg sodium

Mocha "Ice Cream"

Servings: 8

Chocolate and coffee flavors combine to make a delicious recipe for your home ice cream freezer.

5 tbs. cocoa
¾ cup sugar
2 tbs. instant coffee dissolved in 1 tbs. hot water
1 tsp. vanilla
12 ozs. evaporated skim milk
1 cup lowfat buttermilk
1½ cups skim milk

In a large bowl, combine sugar and cocoa. Add remaining ingredients and mix well. Freeze according to your ice cream freezer's directions.

Nutritional information per serving   150 calories, 1 gram fat, .5 grams saturated fat, 3 mg cholesterol, 7 grams protein, 29 grams carbohydrate, 116 mg sodium

Frozen Chocolate Mousse

This is another delicious recipe for your home ice cream freezer. You'll find that making it at home is fun, and also much less expensive than buying a lowfat frozen chocolate mousse from your grocery.

6 tbs. cocoa
1 cup sugar
1 tbs. gelatin
12 ozs. evaporated skim milk

2 cups skim milk
1/4 cup cold water
2 egg whites
2 tsp. vanilla

Dissolve gelatin in 1/4 cup cold water. In a saucepan, mix 3/4 cup sugar and cocoa. Gradually add evaporated skim milk and skim milk. Heat almost to boiling and add gelatin; stir until dissolved. Cool until mixture is room temperature and slightly thickened. In a mixer bowl, beat egg whites until foamy and add remaining 1/4 cup sugar 1 tablespoon at a time until stiff, glossy peaks form. Fold into chocolate mixture and freeze according to your ice cream freezer's directions.

Nutritional information per serving   178 calories, 1 gram fat, .6 grams saturated fat, 3 mg cholesterol, 8 grams protein, 35 grams carbohydrate, 84 mg sodium

Chocolate Orange Sherbet

This is an unusual and delicious flavor combination for sherbet, and one we think your family will ask for again and again.

2 egg whites
2 cups skim milk
2 cups evaporated skim milk
6 ozs. frozen orange juice concentrate, thawed
¾ cup sugar
5 tbs. cocoa

In a large mixing bowl, beat egg whites until foamy. Add skim and evaporated milk, orange juice concentrate, sugar and cocoa; beat well. Freeze according to your ice cream freezer's directions.

Nutritional information per serving   199 calories, 1 gram fat, .5 grams saturated fat, 3 mg cholesterol, 9 grams protein, 39 grams carbohydrate, 101 mg sodium

Pears Belle Helene

Servings: 8

This is an elegant old recipe that we've adapted to be a healthy elegant new recipe.

2 cups apple cider
juice of ½ lemon
1 cinnamon stick
4 firm, ripe pears

1 cup lowfat ricotta cheese
2 tbs. sugar
1 tsp. grated orange rind

In a saucepan, combine cider, lemon juice and cinnamon stick; heat over medium heat until mixture simmers and reduce heat to low. Peel pears and add them to simmering liquid, cover and poach until just tender, about 6 to 8 minutes. Remove from heat and cool in poaching liquid. Drain and chill. In a small bowl, combine ricotta, sugar and orange rind; beat until mixture is smooth and creamy. Chill. Halve and core pears. Fill centers with 2 tbs. ricotta mixture. Place pears cut side down on serving plates. Spoon 2 tbs. chocolate sauce around each and serve.

Chocolate Sauce

1 tsp. gelatin
2 tbs. cold water
1 cup sugar

⅓ cup cocoa
⅓ cup water
1 tsp.. vanilla

Soften gelatin in 2 tbs. cold water for 5 minutes. In a saucepan, combine sugar, cocoa and ⅓ cup water. Cook over medium heat until mixture comes to a boil. Boil 3 minutes, remove from heat and stir in gelatin and vanilla. Stir until gelatin is dissolved. Cool to room temperature.

Nutritional information per serving   152 calories, 4 grams fat, .6 grams saturated fat, 0 mg cholesterol, 4 grams protein, 22 grams carbohydrate, 39 mg sodium

Pots de Creme

Rich-tasting individual chocolate custards are fancy enough for guests or easy enough for a family dessert.

1 cup evaporated skim milk
1 cup skim milk
4 tbs. cocoa

⅓ cup sugar
1 tsp. grated orange rind
1 egg *plus* 2 egg whites

Scald milk in a saucepan over low heat. In a bowl, combine cocoa, sugar, orange rind, egg and egg whites and beat well. Pour scalded milk into chocolate mixture in a slow stream, beating constantly until well combined. Place 4 pot de creme cups or custard cups in an ovenproof casserole large enough to hold them. Fill custard cups with custard and pour boiling water into casserole to half way up the sides of the custard cups. Bake at 350° for 40 minutes. Remove custards; cool to room temperature; then chill or serve warm.

Nutritional information per serving   183 calories, 3 grams fat, 1 gram saturated fat, 66 mg cholesterol, 12 grams protein, 29 grams carbohydrate, 142 mg sodium

---

Chocolate Custard Bread Pudding

Bread puddings used to be a very popular finish to a meal. Here is a variation that may bring back their popularity!

3 tbs. sugar
2 tbs. cocoa
1 egg *plus* 2 egg whites
2½ cups skim milk

1 tsp. vanilla
1 tbs. margarine
4 slices cinnamon raisin bread

In mixing bowl, combine sugar and cocoa. Add egg, egg white, milk and vanilla; beat well. Spread margarine on bread and cut into small cubes. Spray a 7"x11" pan with nonstick cooking spray. Place bread cubes in pan and pour milk mixture over them, letting bread absorb liquid for 5 minutes. Bake at 325° for 25 minutes or until center is set. Cool slightly; serve warm.

Nutritional information per serving 116 calories, 3 grams fat, 1 gram saturated fat, 32 mg cholesterol, 6 grams protein, 16 grams carbohydrate, 62 mg sodium

Chocolate Mocha Pavlova

Servings: 8

Do you recall how Pavlov's dog's mouth watered? **Mocha Pavlova** *will makes yours water, too! Tastes heavenly.*

4 egg whites
¼ tsp. cream of tartar
½ cup sugar

1 tsp. vinegar
1 tsp. vanilla

In a large mixing bowl, beat egg whites until foamy. Add cream of tartar and continue beating on high speed. Add sugar by the tablespoonful, vinegar and vanilla. Beat until firm, glossy peaks form. Do not underbeat. Pile meringue into a mound in a 10" pie pan sprayed with nonstick cooking spray. Bake in a 300° oven for 40 minutes. Cool. During cooling meringue will fall in the center and crack. It will be dry and crisp on the outside and soft and creamy in the center. When cool, spread filling on top and garnish with strawberry slices.

Mocha Filling

1 cup lowfat ricotta cheese
2 tbs. cocoa
2 tbs. sugar

1 tsp. instant coffee dissolved in 1 tsp. water
1 cup sliced strawberries

In a food processor bowl or blender, combine ricotta, cocoa, sugar and dissolved instant coffee; beat well until mixture is smooth and creamy.

Nutritional information per serving   98 calories, 1 gram fat, 0 grams saturated fat, 0 mg cholesterol, 5 grams protein, 18 grams carbohydrate, 62 mg sodium

Chocolate Gingerbread with Custard Sauce

Servings: 16

On a blustery winter evening, there's nothing better than gingerbread—unless it's **Chocolate Gingerbread with Custard Sauce**.

2 cups flour
¼ cup cocoa
⅓ cup sugar
¾ cup dark molasses
⅓ cup unsalted margarine, melted

1 egg plus 2 egg whites
1 tsp. baking soda
1 tsp. *each* ginger and cinnamon
¾ cup water

In a large mixing bowl, combine flour, cocoa, sugar, baking soda, ginger and cinnamon. In another bowl, combine egg and egg whites, molasses, water and margarine; beat well. Add to dry ingredients and beat on medium speed 2 minutes. Pour into a 9"x9" pan sprayed with nonstick cooking spray. Bake at 325° for 45 to 50 minutes or until a cake tester comes out clean. Serve warm, topped with 2 tablespoons of sauce.

Custard Sauce

2 egg whites
2 tbs. sugar

1 cup skim milk
1 tsp. vanilla

In the top of a double boiler, combine and beat well egg whites, sugar and milk. Cook and stir continuously over boiling water until custard thickens and coats a spoon, about 10 minutes. Remove from heat and stir in vanilla. Pour into a bowl, cool slightly and serve warm over gingerbread.

Nutritional information per serving   184 calories, 6.5 grams fat, 1 gram saturated fat, 16 mg cholesterol, 3 grams protein, 29 grams carbohydrate, 70 mg sodium

Beverages

Most of the beverage recipes that follow make individual servings. However, they can be easily increased for party size servings. Always use skim, evaporated skim, or nonfat dry milk powder. Avoid using instant nondairy creamers as they contain the "tropical fats," coconut oil and palm oil, both high in saturated fat. Serve beverages in attractive or unusual glasses and use your imagination to create interesting garnishes. Try serving a freeze or shake in a champagne flute with a fresh flower on top. Give a mug of hot cocoa a festive holiday touch and a minty flavor with a small candy cane for "stirring." Experiment with other combinations of fruit besides those mentioned in these recipes.

Chocolate Shake

This thick, tasty shake is a perfect summer treat.

1 small banana
¼ cup nonfat dry milk powder
½ cup ice water
1 tbs cocoa

2 tsp. sugar
½ tsp. vanilla
1 cup ice cubes

In a food processor or blender, process all ingredients except ice cubes until smooth. Add ice cubes and process until smooth. Serve at once.

Nutritional information per serving 140 calories, 1 gram fat, 0 grams saturated fat, 2 mg cholesterol, 7 grams protein, 29 grams carbohydrate,82 mg sodium

Chocolate Pineapple Frost

Servings: 1

Try any of the pineapple juice blends for a tropical treat.

3 tbs. unsweetened pineapple juice
  concentrate, thawed
⅔ cup water

1 tbs. cocoa
pineapple slice

Shake or whisk juice concentrate, water and cocoa together to dissolve cocoa. Pour in an ice-filled glass. Make 1 cut in pineapple slice; hang on edge of glass.

Nutritional information per serving 113 calories, 1 gram fat, 0 gram saturated fat, 0 mg cholesterol, 2 grams protein, 25 grams carbohydrate, 3 mg sodium

Chocolate Milk

Servings: 1

This is an old favorite with an orange twist.

½ cup evaporated skim milk, chilled
¼ cup ice water
2 tsp. cocoa

2 tsp. sugar
1 tsp. orange juice concentrate

Shake or whisk all ingredients together until smooth.

Nutritional information per serving 151 calories, 1 gram fat, .5 grams saturated fat, 5 mg cholesterol, 11 grams protein, 26 grams carbohydrate, 147 mg sodium

Chocolate Buttermilk Freeze

Servings: 1

Try other frozen fruit for a variety of freezes.

2 tsp. cocoa
1 tbs. honey
2/3 cup lowfat buttermilk

1/2 tsp. vanilla
1/2 cup frozen strawberries

In a food processor or blender, process all ingredients until strawberries are pureed. Serve at once.

Nutritional information per serving   163 calories, 1 gram fat, .5 grams saturated fat, 5 mg cholesterol, 7 grams protein, 33 grams carbohydrate, 173 mg sodium

Chocolate Fruit Smoothie

Servings: 1

This nondairy shake is thick and delicious.

1 small banana
1 fresh peach, peeled or 1/2 cup
 canned peaches in juice, drained

2 tsp. cocoa
1/8 tsp. almond extract
1 cup ice cubes

In a food processor or blender, process all ingredients until fruit is pureed. Serve at once.

Nutritional information per serving   176 calories, 1 gram fat, 0 grams saturated fat, 0 mg cholesterol, 3 grams protein, 44 grams carbohydrate, 4 mg sodium

Mint Chocolate Cooler

Servings: 1

There's just a hint of mint in this cool, refreshing drink.

½ cup evaporated skim milk, chilled
¼ cup ice water
2 tsp. cocoa

2 tsp. sugar
1/16 tsp. mint extract
mint leaves (optional)

Shake or beat all ingredients together until frothy. Fill glass with cracked ice. Add cooler and garnish with mint leaves, if desired.

Nutritional information per serving   144 calories, 1 gram fat, .5 grams saturated fat, 5 mg cholesterol, 11 grams protein, 24 grams carbohydrate, 147 mg sodium

Hot Cherry Chocolate

Servings: 1

The black cherry adds an interesting flavor to this hot chocolate.

1 cup skim milk
1 tbs. cocoa
2 tsp. sugar

1 tsp. black cherry concentrate
⅛ tsp. vanilla

In a saucepan, stir cocoa and sugar into milk. Bring to a boil. Remove from heat, add black cherry concentrate and vanilla; beat until smooth. Serve hot.

Nutritional information per serving   157 calories, 1 gram fat, 1 gram saturated fat, 3 mg cholesterol, 10 grams protein, 27 grams carbohydrate, 128 mg sodium

Malted Milk

Servings: 1

Treat the kids to this lowfat version of malted milk.

2 tsp. cocoa
1 tsp. sugar
2 tsp. malted milk powder

½ cup evaporated skim milk, chilled
½ cup ice water

Shake or beat all ingredients together until frothy. Serve in a frosted glass.

Nutritional information per serving   129 calories, 1 gram fat, .5 grams saturated fat, 5 mg cholesterol, 11 grams protein, 20 grams carbohydrate, 147 mg sodium

Chocolate Cherry Sparkle

Servings: 1

This thirst-quenching drink has a splash of cherry.

1 tbs. black cherry concentrate
2 tsp. sugar

2 tsp. cocoa
1 cup sparkling water

Stir together cherry concentrate, sugar and cocoa until dissolved. Stir mixture into sparkling water. Pour into a glass filled with crushed ice. Serve at once.

Nutritional information per serving   70 calories, 0 grams fat, 0 grams saturated fat, 0 mg cholesterol, 1 gram protein, 16 grams carbohydrate, 1 mg sodium

Chocolate Soda

Servings: 1

A lowfat chocolate syrup and ice milk make this soda easy on the waistline!

2 tbs. chocolate syrup
1/3 cup chocolate ice milk

1 cup sparkling mineral water

Place two tablespoons chocolate syrup in a tall glass. Add ice milk. Fill glass with sparkling water, stirring well.

Chocolate Syrup

1/4 cup water
2 tbs. sugar

3 tbs. cocoa
1/4 tsp. vanilla

Combine water, sugar and cocoa in a saucepan. Bring to a boil, stirring constantly. Cool. Add vanilla.

Nutritional information per serving   102 calories, 3 grams protein, 18 grams carbohydrate, 2 grams total fat, .6 grams saturated fat, 35 mg cholesterol, 35 mg sodium

Banana Split Freeze

Prepare the syrup ahead and let it cool. This recipe makes about ⅔ cup, so save the rest for a lowfat topping for ice milk or frozen yogurt.

½ cup plain lowfat yogurt
1 tbs. nonfat dry milk powder
¼ tsp. vanilla

1 tbs. chocolate syrup
½ medium banana, frozen

In a blender, combine yogurt, dry milk powder, vanilla and chocolate syrup. With the motor running, drop in pieces of frozen banana. Process just until banana is incorporated and mixture is thick and very cold. Serve immediately.

Chocolate Syrup

⅓ cup cocoa
⅓ cup brown sugar

½ cup lowfat buttermilk
1 tsp. vanilla

In a saucepan or microwave dish, combine cocoa, sugar and buttermilk. Heat over low heat until sugar and cocoa are dissolved. Remove from heat and stir in vanilla. Cool. Store unused portion in refrigerator.

Nutritional information per serving   184 calories, 1 gram fat, 0 grams saturated fat, 3 mg cholesterol, 10 grams protein, 37 grams carbohydrate, 264 mg sodium

---

Chocolate Mocha Freeze

Servings: 1

You need only a little advance notice to prepare this hot weather treat.

½ cup plain lowfat yogurt
⅓ cup lowfat buttermilk
1 tsp. instant coffee powder

2 tsp. cocoa
1½ tbs. sugar
1 tbs. nonfat dry milk powder

Combine all ingredients in a blender and blend until smooth. Pour into a 10-ounce glass and place in the freezer until ice crystals begin to form around the edge, about 10 minutes. Remove from freezer and stir well before serving.

Nutritional information per serving 173 calories, 14 grams protein, 26 grams carbohydrate, 1 gram total fat, .7 grams saturated fat, 6 mg cholesterol, 291 mg sodium

Iced Chocolate Mocha

Servings: 1

Iced coffee is a favorite with many people. Use decaffienated and really enjoy it!

⅔ cup chilled coffee
1 tsp. cocoa

1 tsp. sugar
⅓ cup skim milk

In a 12-ounce glass, combine cocoa, sugar and enough milk to make a syrup. Add remaining milk and coffee; stir well. Fill glass with ice cubes and serve.

Nutritional information per serving 36 calories, .4 grams fat, .3 grams saturated fat, 1 mg cholesterol, 3 grams protein, 5 grams carbohydrate, 43 mg sodium

Chocolate Raspberry Frost

Servings: 1

The raspberry sherbet gives a fresh berry taste.

4 oz. raspberry sherbet
½ cup skim milk
1 tbs. chocolate syrup (see **Banana Split Freeze**, page 146)

In a blender, combine all ingredients and blend until smooth. Serve in a 10-ounce glass garnished with a fresh raspberry.

Nutritional information per serving 152 calories, .7 grams fat, .5 grams saturated fat, 5 mg cholesterol, 12 grams protein, 24 grams carbohydrate, 88 mg sodium

Instant Hot Chocolate Mix

Servings: 6

This recipe can easily be increased. Add a teaspoon of cinnamon and a teaspoon of nutmeg for a "Mexican Hot Chocolate" variation, or a tablespoon of instant coffee for a chocolate mocha mix. Hot chocolate mixes make a lovely gift — put in an attractive glass container and share it with a friend.

2 cups nonfat dry milk powder
3 tbs. cocoa
3 tbs. sugar

Mix ingredients together and store in an air-tight container. To serve, add 1/3 cup mix to 8 ounces boiling water and stir to dissolve.

Nutritional information per serving 168 calories, .6 grams fat, .3 grams saturated fat, 5 mg cholesterol, 14 grams protein, 27 grams carbohydrate, 105 mg sodium

Chocolate Peppermint Shake

Servings: 1

Peppermint gives this shake a cool sparkle.

⅓ cup skim milk
1 tbs. nonfat dry milk powder
1 tbs. chocolate syrup (see
  Banana Split Freeze, page 146)

¼ tsp. peppermint extract
½ cup chocolate ice milk
1 peppermint candy, crushed

In a blender, combine all ingredients. Process until smooth. Pour into a glass and sprinkle crushed peppermint on top. Serve immediately.

Nutritional information per serving 177 calories, 8 grams protein, 30 grams carbohydrate, 3 grams total fat, 2 grams saturated fat, 11 mg cholesterol, 133 mg sodium

Index

METRIC CONVERSION CHART

Liquid or Dry Measuring Cup (based on an 8 ounce cup)

1/4 cup = 60 ml
1/3 cup = 80 ml
1/2 cup = 125 ml
3/4 cup = 190 ml
1 cup = 250 ml
2 cups = 500 ml

Liquid or Dry Measuring Cup (based on a 10 ounce cup)

1/4 cup = 80 ml
1/3 cup = 100 ml
1/2 cup = 150 ml
3/4 cup = 230 ml
1 cup = 300 ml
2 cups = 600 ml

Liquid or Dry Teaspoon and Tablespoon

1/4 tsp. = 1.5 ml
1/2 tsp. = 3 ml
1 tsp. = 5 ml
3 tsp. = 1 tbs. = 15 ml

Temperatures

$^{\circ}$F		$^{\circ}$C
200	=	100
250	=	120
275	=	140
300	=	150
325	=	160
350	=	180
375	=	190
400	=	200
425	=	220
450	=	230
475	=	240
500	=	260
550	=	280

Pan Sizes (1 inch = 25 mm)

8-inch pan (round or square) = 200 mm x 200 mm
9-inch pan (round or square) = 225 mm x 225 mm
9 x 5 x 3-inch loaf pan = 225 mm x 125 mm x 75 mm
1/4 inch thickness = 5 mm
1/8 inch thickness = 2.5 mm

Pressure Cooker

100 Kpa = 15 pounds per square inch
70 Kpa = 10 pounds per square inch
35 Kpa = 5 pounds per square inch

Mass

1 ounce = 30 g
4 ounces = 1/4 pound = 125 g
8 ounces = 1/2 pound = 250 g
16 ounces = 1 pound = 500 g
2 pounds = 1 kg

Key   (America uses an 8 ounce cup - Britain uses a 10 ounce cup)

ml = milliliter
l = liter
g = gram
K = Kilo (one thousand)
mm = millimeter
m = milli (a thousandth)
$^{\circ}$F = degrees Fahrenheit

$^{\circ}$C = degrees Celsius
tsp. = teaspoon
tbs. = tablespoon
Kpa = (pounds pressure per square inch)
     This configuration is used for pressure cookers only.

Metric equivalents are rounded to conform to existing metric measuring utensils.

SERVE CREATIVE, EASY, NUTRITIOUS MEALS — COLLECT THEM ALL.

Turkey, The Magic Ingredient
Chocolate Cherry Tortes and Other Lowfat
  Delights
Lowfat American Favorites
Lowfat International Cuisine
The Hunk Cookbook
Now That's Italian!
Fabulous Fiber Cookery
Low Salt, Low Sugar, Low Fat Desserts
What's for Breakfast?
Healthy Cooking on the Run
Healthy Snacks for Kids
Creative Soups & Salads
Quick & Easy Pasta Recipes
Muffins, Nut Breads and More
The Barbecue Book
The Wok
New Ways with Your Wok
Quiche & Soufflé Cookbook
Easy Microwave Cooking
Compleat American Housewife 1787

Cooking for 1 or 2
Brunch
Cocktails & Hors d'Oeuvres
Bread Baking
Meals in Minutes
New Ways to Enjoy Chicken
Favorite Seafood Recipes
No Salt, No Sugar, No Fat Cookbook
The Fresh Vegetable Cookbook
Modern Ice Cream Recipes
Crepes & Omelets
Time-Saving Gourmet Cooking
New International Fondue Cookbook
Extra-Special Crockery Pot Recipes
Favorite Cookie Recipes
Authentic Mexican Cooking
Fisherman's Wharf Cookbook
The Kid's Cookbook
The Best of Nitty Gritty
The Creative Lunch Box

Who do you know that could use one of these popular titles?
Nitty Gritty Cookbooks are available at better gourmet, department and book stores. If you have difficulty
finding them, write to Nitty Gritty at the address below and ask us for our brochure. Buy a few extra copies for
those special gifts this year!

nitty gritty cookbooks Published by Bristol Publishing Enterprises, Inc.
P.O. Box 1737
San Leandro, CA 94577